AF263559

DEATH: THE FINAL ACT OF LOVE

A Practical Guide for Living and Dying Well

Terry W. Barnett, MDiv., J.D., DMin

DEATH: THE FINAL ACT OF LOVE
A Practical Guide for Living and Dying Well

Copyright© 2020 by Terry W. Barnett
All rights reserved.

Although the author and publisher have made every effort to ensure that the information in this book was correct at press time, the author and publisher do not assume and hereby disclaim any liability to any party for any loss, damage, or disruption caused by errors or omissions, whether such errors or omissions result from negligence, accident, or any other cause.

This book is not intended as a substitute for the medical advice of physicians. The reader should consult a physician in matters relating to his or her health, and particularly with respect to any symptoms that may require diagnosis or medical attention.

No part of this publication may be reproduced, stored in a retrieval system, or transmitted in any form by any means electronic, mechanical, photocopying, recording, scanning, or otherwise, except as permitted by the author under the United States Copyright Act, without the prior written consent of the author.

ISBN: 978-0-9915783-7-5

LCCN: 2020918591

Table of Contents

Acknowledgments

Writing and publishing a book is never done in isolation. There have been many people that have contributed to this work. I would like to name just a few. I am deeply indebted to Jean Caughell. Jean's encouragement and friendship made this endeavor a labor of love. Moreover, Jean's proofreading skills helped me to sound smarter than I actually am. I will always be grateful to Camille Gavin. Camille helped me to understand the importance of literary structure and content.

The writing of this book did not begin when I first sat down to write. It began many years ago when I was traveling north on Interstate 5 out of San Diego, California with Carol Preston. Carol shared with me about the love of Jesus Christ and His forgiveness and reconciliation. I will be eternally thankful for Carol's words and faith.

I would like to thank the residents of Rosewood Senior Living Community who enriched my life. They taught me about dying well. Thank you to Cindy Readnower, who walked me through the publishing process. Cindy's experience and competence were invaluable for a first-time author.

My love and thanks to my daughter Chandra Beitner, who showed me firsthand about forgiveness and reconciliation. And thanks to Austen Beitner, my son-in-law who showed me God's grace. I love you both very much.

Last but certainly not least, my parents, Rae Dixon, and L.C. (Pete) Barnett. You will continue to live in my heart.

Author's Note

I wrote this book to help people understand the aspects of dying well. I have shared many stories, including my own. As you read these stories, remember, these are real people with real challenges and struggles. I have learned from so many. Everyone who has shared their lives, deaths, and journeys with me are my guiding light. We can all learn from their journeys. Moreover, I hope you will be inspired and encouraged by how people, with God's help, overcome their weaknesses, anxieties, fears, and insecurities. Please remember that nothing is impossible with God.

The names of patients and other identifying information have been changed to protect their privacy. Some characters are a composite of different individuals I have known. If real names where used, it is with the permission or the information is publicly accessible information.

Preface

As with most books, if your mind and heart are not captivated within the reading of the first several chapters, you are probably not going to finish it. However, I ask you to have patience. Why? Because the focus of this book is extremely important, as it is difficult. We are going to be talking about death and dying; a topic that most people would like to avoid. But we cannot. Our transitioning from this life is absolute. It may be in 30 years, 30 days, 30 minutes. Whenever it is, what you learn in this book will be the greatest gift you give yourself and your loved ones.

My goal is to get you thinking and talking about death, not in some morbid way, but with honest feelings that lead to honest conversations. I want you to imagine as you read this book, that you are taking a journey. It is a journey of discovery. I ask you to read it slowly and prayerfully. Take your time. Go back over and read sections again. Let it sink into your heart. The concepts presented are not difficult. They are easy to understand with your mind. The difficulty comes with moving the concepts from your mind to your heart. If they do not reach your heart, this journey will be fruitless.

As you read, you will realize that I have written it from a Christian perspective. If you are not a Christian, please continue reading. The concepts of forgiveness, reconciliation, and gratitude are embedded in the human nature. You do not have to be a religious person to have these concepts change your life. What I am going to ask you to do in this book, one might argue it should be easier for a person of faith. However, in my research and over two decades of helping people to die well, I am not convinced it is easier. Forgiveness is not easy. Reconciliation takes work. A sense of gratitude is a choice.

So, whether you are a Christian, Muslim, Hindu, Jewish, any other faith tradition, or no faith at all, read this book with your heart. Dying is a human thing. Who knows, maybe you will see the *fingerprints of God* along the way.

What you are about to read in part one is a personal journey. My journey. It is a journey of forgiveness and reconciliation. You might say I have been studying these two concepts most of my adult life. I was first exposed to them at the age of twenty. I was living in San Diego, California. I had been raised in Bakersfield and moved to San Diego the day I turned eighteen. I had been fascinated with the sport of surfing and the beach life since the age of eight when my parents took to me to Catalina Island, off the coast of Long Beach, California. I fell in love with the sea. That love affair continues to this day.

However, my life was about to change significantly. I was drafted into the United States Army in 1972. Needless to say, this was not in my career plans. My life was surfing, not carrying an M-16 in the jungles of Vietnam. As disruptive as my draft notice was, I was willing to do my duty. I entered active duty on June 27, 1972. I had no idea that God had even bigger plans for me.

The reason I am sharing this with you is because what God was about to do in my life would define me throughout my life. It would also begin to prepare me for this moment – the writing of this book. His early "fingerprints" upon my life is the reason I am writing about forgiveness and reconciliation. It was the beginning of my journey in discovering the power of these two concepts. So, part one of this book is my story about how I experienced God's forgiveness and reconciliation. Part two is the practical, hands-on application of that experience.

The application of forgiveness, reconciliation, and gratitude have never been more important. As we continue to live through the COVID-19 pandemic, thousands of people are dying in America. These three concepts are even more important today. My prayer is for you to experience God's fingerprints in your life and the life of your loved ones. The thing about fingerprints is you often cannot see them. You certainly do not see them clearly. But when you put His fingerprints under the microscope of your life experiences, they become clear. As you look back on your life, you can see how He has directed you.

Part one of this book begins God's fingerprints on my life. What I have discovered is His fingerprints continue to mark my life with forgiveness and reconciliation and gratitude. Moreover, His fingerprints will continue all the way to the grave. As you read this book, may you discover the power of God's fingerprints (forgiveness, reconciliation, and gratitude) in your life.

So, let us begin the journey!

Dr. Terry W. Barnett

Part One

Chapter One

THE JOURNEY BEGINS

"Short cuts make long delays."

~ J.R.R. Tolkien

It was a cold winter's day in October. The sun was out but the wind cut like a knife. I was walking the fence line that surrounded three perfectly square buildings. These buildings had no markings except for large numbers above the front doors. Each was the size of a two-story, four-bedroom house. I had measured the distance of the fence line numerous times. It was exactly 1.7 miles from the front gate, around the buildings and back to the gate. I was Private First-Class Terry W Barnett; property of the United States Army and I was on guard duty.

Basic training at Fort Ord, California had gone well enough. I was promoted to platoon guide after four weeks and graduated without too much pain. After graduation and a long weekend, the army shipped me to Fort Dix, New Jersey. I would spend 10 weeks learning a new career. What I did not realize was how hard this new career would be.

Prior to getting drafted in 1972, I was living the ultimate lifestyle. I was surfing every day, partying every night, and generally enjoying all that life had to offer in Southern California. All of that was about to change. Maybe you have heard the statement, "the power of the written word." I never fully understood that statement until I received a one-page letter from my draft board. The letter was not even professionally written. I found two words misspelled and three sentences that were incomplete. I had not done well in my high school English classes, but I expected more from the Federal Selective Service System. At age twenty, it did have the power to change my life.

This one page, poorly written letter informed me that as of June 28, 1972, I would have "GI" stamped clearly on my forehead. And I would wear this facial scarring for the next two years. Say good-bye to the good life and say hello to guard duty.

There are some redeeming features to guard duty. You are outside, at least in this case. The air is crisp and clean and sends your lungs into "shut-down" mode with each breath because of the cold. You get plenty of exercise walking the fence line over, and over, and over. There is time to reflect. We all know how important it is to reflect on one's life, the good decisions, and the bad decisions. It is important to think about the consequences of one's actions. I have always believed the journey of life should bring about more good choices than bad ones. We call this maturing. Back then I was still struggling with not choosing Canada over the army, but that is another story. Then, of course, there is the deep feeling of satisfaction of a job well done. Okay, so I am not surfing every day, but I am serving my country. And my country needs me. Otherwise, why would they teach me how to walk in circles, feed me, and give me a place to call home, and pay me a phenomenal amount of money each month? Seriously, three hundred and thirty-four dollars each month. Really! I felt like I had taken a vow of poverty.

Then all of sudden I had an epiphany. You will probably think I should have realized this long before. But it never occurred to me until that day. I am walking, and freezing, and thinking about my life. As I am reflecting and trying to get my head around what I was doing, it hits me. Blam! I am walking around buildings that have nothing inside. Nothing! I am not protecting state secrets. I am not guarding weapons of mass destruction or nuclear bombs. I am in the middle of Fort Dix, New Jersey, in broad daylight, freezing to death, guarding three buildings that have absolutely no purpose whatsoever! Did I mention freezing? Welcome to Advance Infantry Training and guard duty.

Maybe you have heard that attitude is everything. When Uncle Sam decided to draft me my attitude toward the whole affair was less than stellar. In fact, I had entertained the notion of fleeing to Canada. But I loved my country and wanted to do the right thing. I did, however, have a plan. I would prove to Uncle Sam that I was a poor candidate for the Army.

Within the first several weeks after joining the army, every soldier takes a battery of examinations to determine what they are most suited for. They test your IQ, aptitude, reasoning skills, and your general academic competency. How you perform on these examinations will determine your job.

This was my plan. It was brilliant. I was confident my plan would work, and the army would release me. During the three days of test taking I never read a question. I would just mark any answer my pencil drifted to. Brilliant right? I would appear so stupid they would be forced to send me back to civilian life. What I did not know was the army will not kick you out for being stupid. Here's the army's plan for nonconformist. They train you to be a radio operator with an M16. This would be my new career. I would strap a radio to my back, carry my M16, and run through the jungles of Vietnam. My life expectancy in my new career would be one month. Now that is a brilliant plan.

My training at Fort Dix would last 10 weeks. When I graduated, I would be a full-fledged Radio Telephone Operator (RTO), carrying a PRC-25 field radio on my back, while conducting guerrilla warfare in the jungles of Vietnam. I cannot tell you how excited I was about my new career.

Induction, Fort Ord, CA 1972

I had been at Fort Dix about five weeks when I received my first liberty. I drove up to Boston with some friends for a long weekend. We stayed at a friend's apartment and did what soldiers do when they have liberty. We partied and talked about the good old days. We were all in our twenties, so the good old days were not old. Much of our conversation was about how much we hated the army.

As the weekend rolled on, our bewitching hour was getting closer and closer. Our liberty passes clearly stated we had to be back on base prior to midnight on Sunday. The thought of returning was overwhelming. I missed California and my life. So, I came up with a new plan. Now, you might be thinking that my ability to make long-range plans was not one of my strong suits. And you would be right. Nevertheless, while sitting in an apartment in Boston, I decided to fly back to California and go surfing.

Was I thinking clearly? Probably not. But this was my new plan. I would fly out of Boston on Monday afternoon and return to my life in California. It was a good plan except for one thing. Can you see where this is going? When I failed to arrive back at Fort Dix on

Sunday night, the army would classify me as "absent without leave." I would be AWOL! Did I care? Well, yes and no. Had I thought through what I was going to do after returning to California? Of course, I was going surfing. Had I thought about Fort Leavenworth and prison? Not really. I was not thinking long-term. I was in the moment. And the moment was all I wanted. So, I got on a plane and flew to San Francisco and forgot all about the army. All I cared about was being on the West Coast- sand, surf, and freedom. What I did not realize was that my new freedom would be short lived.

After arriving in San Francisco, I hitch-hiked down to the central coast near Pismo Beach and stayed with friends. I was back in California. I was back in the good life. For the next several days, I hung-out, surfed, and tried to forget about the army. I decided to travel down to San Diego. I had more friends and surf spots to visit. But the weight of my circumstances started to crush me. The more I tried to run, the heavier my burden felt. Let's face it; I was AWOL from the army. During times of war, soldiers were shot for this offense. Would I be shot? Would I go to prison? Would I be forced to leave the country? My life was spinning out of control. I was in crisis. I had no idea where to turn.

For nine days I had been free of the army. But inside I was being held captive by fear, isolation, and guilt. I was a deserter. The more I thought about my choice to run away, the more I realized the trouble I was in. Under the *Uniform Code of Military Justice*, my offense was a felony. Even though Vietnam was considered a "conflict" and not a war, the punishment for desertion would be severe. It would involve a general court-martial, dishonorable discharge, and a maximum of five years in prison. What had I been thinking? Had I lost my mind? Apparently. But what was done was done. I could not change the past.

A friend was driving me back to the central coast in her VW bus. We were traveling north on the San Diego Freeway. I was sobbing and afraid. As tears were pouring down my face, my friend reached over and gently put her hand on my shoulder. She said, "Terry, I know you are frightened, but I know someone who can help."

As we drove north on Interstate 5 out of San Diego, I felt broken. My stomach was in knots. I thought I would throw-up. I do not think I even felt her hand on my shoulder. It took a few seconds for my brain to register what my friend had said. What could she possibly mean? How could someone help me? I was AWOL from the army. No one could help me. My life was in shambles. The only thing I had to look forward to was a dishonorable discharge and prison. Through my tears I heard the words again, "Terry, I know someone who can help." This time her words clearly registered in my brain. I caught my breath and tried to respond. When I looked her way, I notice her mouth moving but there was no sound. Was she praying?

When I could finally speak, I asked, "What do you mean, you know someone who can help?" As I was trying desperately to regain my composure, my friend pulled to the side of the freeway and stopped. She once again placed her hand on my shoulder. I figured she was about to tell me she knew a good lawyer, but what she said next, I was completely unprepared for. She spoke with a gentle firmness and a conviction that was soothing. She said, "Terry, there is only one person who can help you, his name is Jesus Christ."

I knew Carol was a Christian. We had met through mutual friends and I had grown to respect her. She was easy to be around. Our relationship had been based entirely on friendship. When I heard the name Jesus Christ, the world seemed to stop, but my mind was racing. Doesn't she know I am not religious? How can a dead religious guy do anything for me? These questions and many more went through my mind in a split-second. Then to my amazement, I heard the words, "How can Jesus help me?" come out of my mouth. I heard myself ask the question. Had I completely lost it? The stress must be affecting my reason. Did I really say that?

Carol told me that God loved me. And if I were willing to ask God to forgive my sins, He would do it and I would be a new person. She then quoted the Bible. I did not know it at the time, but I would later memorize the verse she was about to quote. She said, *"Anyone who belongs to Christ has become a new person. The old life is gone; a new life has begun!"* All I heard was new person. This is exactly what I needed. I needed to be a new person. The old me had not done very well.   Something was happening to me. A tiny seed of faith was beginning to grow. It did not seem so stupid after all. Then she quoted John 3:16, something about God's son dying for me and giving me eternal life. But, in all honesty, all I could think about was being a new person —a different person. If God could do that for me, then count me in.

As we sat on the side of the freeway with the world still whizzing by, my world had stopped. All I could think about was being new. My mind was in overdrive. Could this really be true? Did God love me? Did Jesus die for my sins? There were so many sins. Then there was the army. How would God fix that? At that moment, Carol, once again reached over and touched my shoulder. She said, "Terry, God really does love you, and His Son really did die to forgive your sins, and you really can become a new person." As she paused allowing her words to sink in, she asked if I would pray with her to receive Christ as my Lord and Savior. I did not know exactly what that meant, but I said, "Yes."

As we continued driving back to San Luis Obispo, I realized I felt different. I felt calm. I was no longer weeping. I know this sounds weird, but I felt warm inside. My circumstances had not changed. I was still very AWOL. I was still facing a court-marshal. And I was still facing going to prison. What had changed? In the few seconds it took to pray to receive Christ, God had become real to me. It felt like a weight had been lifted off my chest. I would later learn the Holy Spirit takes up residence in every new believer. The Holy Spirit had calmed my heart and I was no longer afraid. I still knew I was in serious trouble, but I felt so calm. I could not explain it, but I knew God would get me through everything. My life would be forever changed. I had become that new person.

When we arrived in San Luis Obispo, Carol introduced me to her pastor. His name was Rev. Edward Lansbury. He was in his mid-seventies but looked like he was sixty. Pastor Lansbury was a big man and in good shape. He stood six feet four inches and had thick black hair. I particularly remember his hair because I always wanted hair like his. Besides the hair, Pastor Lansbury had amazing blue eyes, full of kindness. When he talked to you it seemed like you had his complete attention. No one else mattered. And when he spoke to you, you wanted to listen. He was a man full of wisdom and understanding.

Pastor Lansbury had been ordained in the Assemblies of God tradition and had pastored in San Luis Obispo for twenty years. After several hours of telling him my story, he invited me to stay with him and his wife until we could figure out what to do. It was a small detail, but I could see God at work. I had friends in the area, but they were part of my old life. This new person wanted to do what Mary had done when Jesus visited her and her sister, Martha. at their home. I wanted to sit at the feet of Jesus and listen. I knew Pastor Lansbury was the next best thing to sitting with Jesus. Over the next ten days I had a crash course in Discipleship 101. I was reading the Bible, memorizing scripture, going to church, and enjoying the presence of the Holy Spirit.

Mrs. Lansbury was an extraordinary woman as well. In her early seventies, she was a Pentecostal Mother Teresa. I do not believe Mrs. Lansbury ever wrote a book, started an orphanage, or cared for the dying like Mother Teresa; she was, however, kindness on steroids. For the ten days I lived in her home, she treated me like a son. She gave wise counsel, godly correction when needed, and could she cook. She had grown up in the south and her fried chicken knew their roots. Best fried chicken I ever ate. During one of the fried chicken dinners I enjoyed (there were several) while living there, Pastor Lansbury asked me a life-changing question. This should not have come as a surprise; he was always asking these types of questions. As I was about to sink my teeth into a golden-brown piece of southern fried chicken, Pastor Lansbury said, "Terry, I think you should consider being baptized, what do you think?"

I had read about John the Baptist. And I knew Jesus had gotten baptized, but I was not sure how to respond. To be honest, at that moment I was more interested in the piece of chicken in my mouth. I was hungry and not ready to re-engage my brain with such a deep theological question. Midway through dinner, however, I was able to think. After Pastor Lansbury explained what baptism meant, he told me to read Matthew 28:19. I did not have my Bible handy, but no matter. In the Lansbury house there was always one close by. He turned and reached behind where he was sitting and pulled one out of the cabinet, handed it to me and said read Matthew 28, verses 19-20, so I did. Jesus was speaking with his disciples, *"Therefore, go and make disciples of all the nations, baptizing them in the name of the Father and the Son and the Holy Spirit. Teach these new disciples to obey all the commands I have given you."*

With a full stomach, I told Pastor Lansbury I wanted to be baptized. So, after several more days of study and prayer the day came. I had asked Pastor Lansbury if it would be okay to be baptized in the ocean and not in the church. He knew about my love affair with the sea. We had talked about how I enjoyed the ocean as my personal playground. So, in early October, a small caravan left First Assembly of God Church in San Luis Obispo and drove halfway between Avila Beach and Port San Luis. When we arrived, I was having second thoughts. How can I say this? It was cold, really cold. It was foggy, the sky was overcast, the air temperature was hovering just above 56 degrees, and the water temperature was colder than the air. I was having flashbacks to guard duty at Fort Dix. Pastor Lansbury kept saying, "Come on, come on, it's not getting any warmer."

It was not until the next day I found out how much Pastor Lansbury was enjoying himself during my baptism. He had brought a wetsuit. I, on the other hand, had not even thought about the weather. As he was suiting up, I was standing near the water's edge shivering. Just before it was time to enter the water, Pastor Lansbury wanted to pray. He was known for long and eloquent prayers. And of course, any other time that would be wonderful. But not now, please God not now.

About three minutes into what was beginning to sound like a ten-minute prayer, easy, Pastor Lansbury started laughing. He was laughing hard, almost uncontrollably. I did not know what to think. Was he having a seizure? Should I call for the paramedics? Did I mention he had a sick sense of humor? I am so cold. I am afraid my chattering teeth might break a crown loose. When Pastor Lansbury's laughing slowed to where he could regain some physical composure, he reached down and pulled a wetsuit from his backpack. He tossed it to me, still belly laughing, and said, "Hey Terry, you look cold, maybe you should wear this." I never really saw the humor.

We walked into the water until it was waist high. I had done a brief run through at the church, so I knew what to expect. As we stood in the water, Pastor Lansbury asked me if I had accepted Jesus Christ as my Lord and Savior. I respond with "Yes." He asked me if I had repented of my sins and I again said, "Yes." Then I heard him say, "Terry, based on your confession of faith, I now baptize you in the name of the Father, the Son, and the Holy Spirit." Then I was under water. It did not seem so cold now.

The next day I was having lunch with the man who nearly let me die from hypothermia. He was still laughing every time he thought about it. But then he got a serious look on this face and said, "We need to talk about the army." I knew he was right. I wanted to avoid it, but time was running out. Pastor Lansbury continued, "Terry, there is only one honorable thing to do." I knew what he was going to say; I had already come to the same conclusion. He said, "You must turn yourself in." We decided to drive up to Fort Ord the following day. It was a four-hour journey, but he was kind enough to drive me.

Chapter Two

WHO SAYS MIRACLES DO NOT EXIST

"There are only two ways to live your life. One is as though nothing is a miracle. The other is as though everything is a miracle."

~ Albert Einstein

We arrived at Fort Ord at 11:30 a.m. It was a cloudless day with a nice ocean breeze blowing in from Monterey Bay. I had completed my basic training just two months prior. Basic training left me with few good memories except for being near the ocean. I knew however, this experience would be the worst of all. I was about to turn myself in for desertion. How well could it possibly go? Within the next sixty minutes I would be handcuffed, chains put on my ankles, and placed into an interrogation cell. I would probably be questioned all weekend about my last 14 days. Maybe I should re-think this? Maybe Canada would be a better option? Is there surf in Canada?

We found the Provost Marshal's Office (PMO), which is like the police department for a city. And like cities, each army post has an office. The office consists of law enforcement officers (military police), criminal investigators working in the Criminal Investigation Division (CID), and numerous administrative roles. The larger the army post, the larger the office. Fort Ord's office was huge. I knew this, because during basic training you receive a class on the history and operation of the Provost Marshal's Office. It was very intimidating. These guys were not drafted. They joined. They are army all the way. So here I am, a surfer, a draftee, a deserter. I am in serious trouble. My life is beginning to flash before my eyes. I am hoping there is life after death because I am about to find out.

Over the double-wide doors leading into the building are the words, *Office of the Provost Marshal*, (all who enter do so at their own risk). Okay, I added that last part, but I was sure it was true. As we entered the building, I noticed my knees felt strange. They felt like rubber. I was worried I might wet myself. We walked up to the window and there stood a massive human being. He must have been a weightlifter; his arms looked like the size of a small tree and his uniform was impeccable. And I could tell he hated surfers. I stood directly in front of the window and Pastor Lansbury stood off to my right. I did not have any spit so the first couple of words I muttered were not audible. I knew Pastor Lansbury was praying for me, so I swallowed again, and said, "My name is Terry Barnett, Private First Class and I am a deserter."

The sergeant behind the window never looked my direction until he heard the word deserter. As I stood at the window, I could see a crossword puzzle and a pencil in his right hand. Standing there, trying to put syllables together, he paid no attention until he heard the "D" word. He raised his head and looked me square in the eyes, and said, "What did you say?" I stepped back several inches and repeated my name, rank, and that I was AWOL from Fort Dix, New Jersey. As my words trailed off my lips, the sergeant leaned forward. His massive frame seemed larger than before. He asked me my name one more time and my social security number. Then he said, "Have a seat over there," and pointed to several chairs next to the wall. I walked over and took a seat. As I looked back his way, he was still staring at me. His eyes were penetrating.

He turned and walked away. I watched him go to another office and knew my life was about to end. As I sat there with Pastor Lansbury, I didn't have much to say. I knew my friend was still praying for me, which was very reassuring. But I also knew my life was about to radically take a new course. It felt like I had been sitting there for hours. When I looked up at the clock, it had only been four minutes. Then, the sergeant and another man walked out of the office. I stood up but couldn't move. Pastor Lansbury stood next to me. Both men walked through a door adjacent to the window where I first met the military's version of the Hulk. Both men came and stood directly in front of me. The other man was a captain, so I stood at attention.

His name was Captain John Murphy. He was the Assistant Provost Marshal. Standing next to the sergeant, he seemed to disappear. He was short, standing 5' 5", with graying hair, and a stocky build. Captain Murphy was well-groomed and carried himself in a professional manner. He seemed serious, but not too serious.

I waited to be handcuffed and shackled and placed into custody. Captain Murphy's mouth was moving but I could not hear. My mind was in over-drive. Finally, something registered in my brain. The captain had asked me my name again. I told him and he said to have a seat. Both men walked back to the same office and disappeared for another ten minutes. I knew this could not be good. They were probably planning their strategy on how to break me. I was convinced I would be tortured with either electricity or waterboarding. Ten minutes passed and only Captain Murphy returned. Waiting, I realized I had read too many Ian Fleming novels. The captain walked through the door and approached me. As I started to stand up, he said, "Private Barnett, just stay seated. We need to talk." As I sat there, I was not prepared for what was about to happen.

Captain Murphy pulled a chair around in front of me and sat down. As I sat there with Pastor Lansbury waiting to hear the words, "Under the Uniform Code of Military Justice, I am placing you under arrest for desertion." Instead, I heard the words, "Could you come back on Monday?" It was a good thing I was sitting down. As his words registered in my brain, my mouth began to drop. Apparently, the captain could see the surprised look on my face. He looked at me with kindness and repeated the question, "Can you return on Monday morning?"

I looked over at Pastor Lansbury. He had a confused look on his face too. Before I could get any words out of my mouth, the captain continued. He stated, "Private Barnett, our holding facility is under construction, so I have no place to keep you. I need you to promise me you will return on Monday; can you do that?" Pastor Lansbury looked at me, then at the captain and said, "Yes, I will bring Private Barnett back on Monday morning." I was glad Pastor Lansbury had responded because I was still unable to form any words. As we drove back to Santa Cruz, we were both speechless. As I thought about what the captain had said, I realized I had experienced God's intervention. This was the first of many godly interventions I would enjoy over the next two years.

We arrived early on Monday morning. I said farewell to Pastor Lansbury, and with tears in my eyes, we hugged and shook hands. As I watched him drive away, my heart was heavy. I did not know it then, but I would never see him again. By three o'clock that afternoon I was flying aboard a military transport to Fort Dix, New Jersey. I had been absent without leave for fourteen days.

I was never placed in handcuffs or shackles like I thought. But I was treated as someone of suspicion. The flight crew seemed indifferent. I was just another soldier hopping a flight. When we arrived at Fort Dix, I was certain I would be hogtied and beaten. Of course, I would not be beaten, but I was sure I would be taken into custody like any military prisoner. Once on base, I was told to report to my barracks and remain in my room. I was waiting for the handcuffs. But it never happened. I was shocked and a little disappointed. I was a criminal.

I had been AWOL for fourteen days. I was a serious threat to our nation's security. Often, what we think in our heads is larger than real life. When I returned to my barracks, I was informed I needed to report to the company commander the following morning.

After a long, sleepless night, I was up by 5:00 a.m. I was scheduled to report at 9:00 a.m. but I did not want to be late. I spent the morning in prayer and getting ready for my appearance. I had never met Lieutenant Colonial (LTC) William B. Bartlett, but I had heard stories. And the stories that I had heard did not make me feel secure about my future. I knew LTC Bartlett was army all the way. He had attended West Point and graduated with honors. He was a veteran of Korea and Vietnam. I was in serious trouble.

It was 8:50 a.m. when I arrived at company headquarters. I reported to the company clerk, who looked at me with disgust. Apparently, he knew I had been AWOL. With a stupid smirk on his face, he told me to have a seat and LTC Bartlett would see me soon. Did he know something I did not? His phone rang and he immediately looked at me, with that same smirk. He set the receiver down and motioned me through the door that was to his left. This was the moment. Even though the Provost Marshall's Office at Fort Ord had treated me with respect and decency, I was sure this was the end. LTC Bartlett was responsible for every soldier under his command. Soldiers going AWOL would reflect poorly on him to his superiors. Once again, I had a gut-wrenching feeling something terrible was going to happen.

I walked through the door and there he was, sitting behind a massive desk. Even sitting behind the desk, he was intimidating. He was a large man with a square face and a short haircut. There were so many ribbons on his uniform, I could not count them. He was chewing the remnant of a cigar. He could have been the army's poster boy. He just looked army.

He was working on something and did not look up. I walked to the front of his desk and reported, "Private Barnett, reporting as ordered, sir." I stood at attention for what seemed like an hour. Finally, LTC Bartlett looked up. When his eyes caught my eyes, he said, "Well, private, it seems you have enjoyed a small vacation." I stated, "Yes, sir." I was not sure what to say beyond that. But there was something about his eyes, besides being bright blue, there was a kindness about them. So, I continued telling him my story. He almost seemed interested.

As I stood there, telling him about becoming a Christian, with my knees shaking and my voice cracking, he listened patiently. I told LTC Bartlett about how I fell in love with Jesus and all the changes that had taken place. I was still convinced that God wanted me out of the army. As I would discover, new believers lacking maturity often come to the wrong conclusion. As I stood before this man, who held the power to send me to prison for a very long time, I confidently stated, "I know God wants me out of the army, no matter what."

With a sparkle in his eye, LTC Bartlett stated, "Private Barnett, if you choose to leave the army before your enlistment is up, you will receive a dishonorable discharge. And this will follow you the rest of your life. Are you sure, you want to leave under those conditions?" I did not want a dishonorable discharge, but I did not want to be in the army either. Surely, if God loved me the way I believed, He had a plan that did not involve the army. As I stood there, I boldly proclaimed that I wanted out of the army, period! LTC Bartlett thought for a minute, and then said, "Private Barnett, since you have become a Christian, what about working in an army chapel?"

I did not know what to say. I just stood there. LTC Bartlett must have sensed my confusion because he continued, "What about working as a Chaplain's Assistant in a military chapel?" "You would work with an army chaplain and assist him with his pastoral duties." I thought for a moment and responded with, "Absolutely." A Chaplain's

Assistant or court martial? It was a no brainer. I certainly did not want a dishonorable discharge, but I did not want to hump a radio through the jungles of Vietnam either. Once again, God's presence was evident. LTC Bartlett stated he would send a request asking for a transfer to Chaplain's Assistant school immediately.

Of course, there was still the issue of being AWOL. LTC Bartlett informed me I would still be subject to an Article 15 under the Code of Military Justice. An Article 15 is a non-judicial punishment with no lasting consequence. It is like an in-house slap on the wrist. It would appear on my discharge papers, but I could still leave the army with an honorable discharge. I thanked him and rendered a heartfelt salute, then left his office.

A week later I appeared in court and received an Article 15 with the following sanctions: I was confined to my barracks for one month. I would be allowed to travel to my workstation and trainings but could not leave the base. In addition, I was ordered to forfeit a month's wages. Seemed a small price to pay for being AWOL fourteen days. It had to be a God thing. Several days later, however, I received bad news. My military test scores were so low it was impossible to quality for a job as a Chaplain's Assistant. I was kicking myself for not taking the Army's entrance exams seriously. Not reading the questions and marking any answer that my pen fell upon had come back to haunt me. As far as the army was concerned, my IQ was strikingly similar to a single-cell amoeba.

I was in my eighth day of confinement when I was ordered to report to LTC Bartlett's office. I already knew why he wanted to see me. I was sure my future held only two options. Carrying a radio on my back or leave the army with a dishonorable discharge, neither were good career options. There was no waiting this time. LTC Bartlett's door was open and the clerk motioned me to go in. I walked in and stood at attention in the same place I had a few days earlier. Without any fanfare, LTC Bartlett said, "you have a problem." "Yes sir, I know," was my reply. As I started to speak again, LTC Bartlett raised his hand, indicating he wanted me to shut up. I promptly did.

He was quiet for a moment, and then said, "Private, what the hell is wrong with you? Your test scores place you in the 68 percentile which means you're feeble-minded." He stood up and with a voice like a truck horn, yelled, "Are you feeble-minded, son?" I was not sure he wanted me to respond, so I whispered, "No sir." He yelled back, "What?" I retorted with, "NO SIR." He seemed satisfied with my answer and sat back down. I then told him the story of my brilliant plan to intentionally sabotage my entry exams. I think I saw a glimmer of a smile cross his face. He then blurted out, "Well, private, I can assure you with an IQ of 68 you will never be assigned to Fort Hamilton and Chaplain Assistant's School. In fact, I'm not sure you could peel potatoes."

I had never felt more stupid than I did at that moment. LTC Bartlett sat there shaking his head, back and forth. He was not saying a word, but his body language was yelling, "You dummy." After several minutes that felt like hours, LTC Bartlett looked at me and said, "Ok, I want you to go back to your barracks and remain there until Thursday. It was Tuesday. Report back to me at 0900 hours on Thursday morning. Are we clear?" "Yes sir," I said, as I raised my right hand for a salute. I turned and left his office.

Those were the longest two days of my life. I had nothing to do but sit around in my room. My training had been suspended pending the outcome of my case. Even though my court appearance had come and gone, I was still in limbo. It was clear I would not be assigned to Fort Hamilton for Chaplain Assistant School, but LTC Bartlett wanted to see me tomorrow at 0900 hours. I wondered why. Maybe he wanted to yell at me again. I hoped that was not the reason. I already felt lower than whale dung. Maybe he would release me from the army with an honorable discharge. Really! Now I knew I was losing it. I was thinking and trying too hard to figure everything out. What I needed to do was pray.

As I was sitting on my bunk, I remembered something Pastor Lansbury had told me. He said, "When you are worried about something, look up Philippians 4:6 in the New Testament." I reached over to the nightstand and picked up my Bible. I turned to Philippians and read, *"Don't worry about anything; instead, pray about everything. Tell God what you need and thank him for all he has done."* As soon as I read that, I had this feeling I should pray. I slid off the bunk unto my knees. As I knelt beside my bunk, I asked God to turn the impossible into possible.

As the shadows grew deeper in my room, I thought back on my journey so far. I remembered how Carol had talked with me about Jesus and how I had come to faith. I remembered showing up at Fort Ord and being told to come back Monday. I remembered how LTC Bartlett seemed to care about my future. It had been twenty-eight and one-half days since this journey had begun, but in some ways, it seemed much longer. Emotionally, it had been a roller-coaster ride. As I laid on my bunk thinking about my life, I felt at peace. I knew God was there. As my eyes closed, I wondered what tomorrow would bring.

When you are in the army, you become accustomed to rising early. "Reveille" is played at sunrise. You can hear it throughout the base. At the same time "Reveille" is played, the American flag is raised. If you are outside at this hour, you stop and render a salute until the music stops. You always face towards the flag or music. It is an army tradition. Usually I was not outside at this time, unless on guard duty. This morning, "Reveille" was my alarm clock. When the music pierced my ears, my eyes immediately opened. Once my mind focused, I started to pray, "Lord, you know this is a big day. I am asking you to go before me. Lord, I want only your will. I have no idea how you might work this out, but I am going to trust you. Help me to trust you. Please show me what to do. Amen."

LTC Bartlett was in the office by 0600 hours every morning. I had heard this from First Sergeant Sean O'Leary. It was First Sergeant O'Leary's job to keep 236 soldiers in line. He ran the day-to-day operations of the company. Since graduating from basic training, I had been assigned to Fort Dix for Advanced Individual Training (AIT). It was First Sergeant O'Leary's responsibility to oversee my training as a radio operator. He took his responsibilities seriously. Since going AWOL, I had fallen, way down, on his respect meter. But it was not just me. First Sergeant O'Leary did not like anyone, however I was at the top of his dislike list. And he wanted me to know.

Knowing LTC Bartlett would be in his office early, I thought I should be as well. It was a fifteen-minute walk from my barracks to his office. After breakfast and some last-minute touch-up of my uniform, I was off. I was walking down the hall with focused intent, when I heard, "Private Barnett, get your ass in here." I turned around and First Sergeant O'Leary was standing by a door, pointing inside. "Now," he growled. As I walked into the office, he told me to sit down. I didn't sit immediately; instead, I started to tell him I had an appointment with LTC Bartlett. But before I could get two words out, he slammed his desk with his hands and yelled, "Shut up." I sat down. He took a long breath, and then said, "Barnett, I don't like you. You have no respect for the uniform or what it represents. I want you to know, I am going to make your life a living hell. When you went AWOL, it was like you slapped me in the face. How dare you. You have at least four to six months left in your training and I assure you, it will be the hardest time you have ever done. Now, get out of here."

As I got up to leave, I could see the veins in his neck bulging. I thought he might have a heart attack. I never said a word. I thought of Jesus and how he had stood silent before his persecutors. In my case, First Sergeant O'Leary was right. I had disrespected the uniform. Many men wearing the same uniform had died in Vietnam. I knew O'Leary had been back in the states only six months. He had done two tours in Vietnam. Men had died. Good men. No wonder he hated me so much. As I walked to post headquarters, I felt ashamed. I decided to take everything First Sergeant O'Leary threw at me and I would do it with honor.

I walked up the steps trying not to slip, since it was October, a month when New Jersey usually has snow and ice. Today was no exception. I keep wondering what might happen in my meeting with LTC Bartlett. I was sure there were only two options: continue my current path of training or leave the army with a dishonorable discharge. I would have to choose. As I thought about these options, I felt confused. As I walked into headquarters, I started to pray. "Lord, I need your help. What should I do? I ask you to give me the courage to make the right decision, in Jesus' name." LTC Bartlett's clerk was not at his desk, so I took a seat. LTC Bartlett's door was closed, but I could hear his voice booming. He sounded frustrated.

As I sat outside his office, I felt like a schoolboy who was waiting to see the principal. My mind drifted back to my junior high days. I was in seventh grade and sitting in the school office for being too talkative. This was not my first offense. I had been in the office numerous times for the same problem. I had a disease; I could not help it. It was called "motor-mouth" disease. Being the class clown was hard work, but I excelled at it. Like any other career, if you wanted to be successful, there was a price. In my case, the price was being sent to the principal's office. Usually, this meant I would sit for an hour in time-out. Today however, would be different. On this day, I would receive corporal punishment. A paddle planted firmly and squarely on my butt.

When LTC Bartlett's clerk walked in, my stroll down memory lane came to a screeching halt. He walked pass me without any acknowledgment, went to his desk, sat down, and started looking through the base phone directory. He was a short man with red hair and freckles. As I watched him, LTC Bartlett's door swung open and he motioned me in. I walked up to his desk and stood at attention. LTC Bartlett told me to take a seat. He had never asked me to sit down before. I wondered what it meant. I knew it could not be good. LTC Bartlett was still standing. As our eyes met, his face seemed particularly rigid. He looked like he was in pain. As I braced myself, I could feel my heart begin to race. This was the moment. It is all over.

What I did not know was LTC Bartlett fancied himself an actor. I was later told how he would play tricks on his staff by pretending to be angry. As he sat down, glaring at me with his penetrating eyes, a huge smile came across his face. It was like his entire face changed. He reminded me of the Cheshire cat in Alice in Wonderland. He had the same mischievous look. I was stunned. I just sat there, unsure of what to do. After LTC Bartlett enjoyed the moment, he finally said, "Private Barnett, I have a deal for you." I responded, "Yes, sir." As he talked about army protocol, I felt like we had been friends for years. Besides being an amateur actor, LTC Bartlett was a Christian. I did not know it at the time, but he had been a believer for many years. After telling me about all the rules the army had, he said, "Private Barnett, I had to pull some strings, and the army is going to allow you to redo your exams. If your scores are within the necessary range, you will be reassigned to Fort Hamilton and Chaplain Assistant School."

I was speechless. I knew my mouth was open, but I just sat there. LTC Bartlett finally said, "How do you feel about that?" I could feel the tears beginning to form in my eyes. Through my amazed bewilderment, I said, "Yes sir, I would very much like to retake my exams." LTC Bartlett looked at me still grinning, but more serious now, and said, "Good." As we continued to talk, he told me to report to the training center at 0800 hours the following day. I stood to go and gave LTC Bartlett a heart-felt salute. He returned my salute, and then put his hand out. As I shook his hand, I said, "Thank you sir."

He wished me good luck and I left his office. I never saw LTC Bartlett again.

It had been two weeks since I had returned to Fort Dix. I could hardly believe what had happened during that time. God was answering my prayers. My re-examinations went well. I scored in the 98th percentile and was reassigned to Fort Hamilton. The following Monday, I left Fort Dix, never to return. I had a new life. God was answering prayers in amazing ways. I had no idea what was in store for me, but I was learning that pursuing God was an adventure and I was excited. The bus trip from Fort Dix to Fort Hamilton took just over two hours. When I stepped off the bus, it was lunch time. After lunch I reported to my new company.

Fort Hamilton is located in Brooklyn, New York, just below the Verrazano-Narrows Bridge. I had been accepted into the Chaplain Assistant Basic Course. It was eight-weeks of intensive training on assisting Army Chaplains with their ministries to soldiers and family members. My training involved three specific areas: non-religious counseling, administrative duties, and the willingness to bear arms to protect the chaplain. For the first time, I felt excited to be part of the army. Even if I was sent to Vietnam, I was ready to serve. I remembered First Sergeant O'Leary and swore to myself that I would never dishonor my uniform again. I had a new passion. I had fallen in love with Jesus and my desire to follow him was growing every day.

My class was larger than most, sixty-three soldiers. We worked hard during our eight-week program, only losing six. We started each morning at 0630 hours and did not stop until 1830 hours in the evening. This went on six days a week. The intensity of the training was very demanding. I had never been a good student. My middle school and high school experiences were disasters. I was bored in school. And my boredom led to being distracted easily. I was always in some form of trouble, usually for not paying attention and talking too much. This experience was different. I was engaged and focused.

It was the first time I had done well academically. I realized I could excel by using my mind. I graduated at the top of my class. The day after graduation, my company commander advised the class we would be receiving orders to our final duty stations within the week. The scuttlebutt going around was that most of the class would be going to Vietnam.

During my last week at Fort Hamilton, there was not much to do. I was waiting for orders and bouncing around New York City. I went to several Broadway shows and four museums during the week. The off-Broadway production of *Godspell* was particularly delightful. Even with all the activity during the week, it was impossible not to think about where I might be going. It was Friday morning and orders were handed out. As I looked at the envelope, I had a knot in my throat. I opened it and saw the words…South Korea.

As I thought about South Korea, I tried to imagine what it would be like. I had eighteen months left to complete my enlistment. I would be shipping out on Monday. Today was Friday. I was a full-fledged Chaplain's Assistant and I was ready to serve my country. I was not sure South Korea was better than Vietnam, but by next week I would be working for a Chaplain halfway around the world. My plan for the weekend was to rest and pray. I did both. Praying was coming easier and I enjoyed listening to God's small, still voice in my heart. It was comforting. As I thought about being stationed in South Korea, I had such a peace. I knew God was for me and not against me. I was ready.

Monday morning, I reported to company headquarters to receive my final orders and ship out. When I entered the waiting area, there were six other Chaplain's Assistants waiting. I had trained with them over the last eight weeks. One of them, Kent Stacy, had become a dear friend. Kent was an amazing guy. He played the guitar and had a beautiful baritone voice. During our training at Fort Hamilton, we would gather in the chapel after training and sing praise songs. Kent was one of those guys that everyone liked. He was tall, handsome, and built like a rock. He would do anything for anyone. Kent wanted to be a medical missionary when he got out of the army. I had no doubt that would be exactly what he would do.

As we were standing there talking about the last eight months, First Sergeant Mackey appeared in the doorway. As he was calling out names, I noticed my heart beginning to beat faster. I had had so many amazing moments since becoming a Christian, and I knew this was about to be another. Then I heard, "Private Barnett." I stepped forward and took the envelope. I felt like I needed to sit down, but I stood there and opened my orders. When I glanced at the box that read "duty station," I saw the words, Fort Hood, Texas. I was going to Texas. I wondered what happened to South Korea. I had been assigned to Alfa Company, 227th Aviation Battalion, First Cavalry Division at Fort Hood. Wow! I could not believe it.

When I looked over at Kent, I noticed a smile on his face. Curious, I walked over and asked him where he had been stationed. Kent replied, "Texas, Fort Hood, Texas." My mouth dropped. I could not believe it. I said, "I'm going to Texas too." We just stared at each other. We both broke out in hilarious laughter. Kent said, "I have been assigned to Bravo Company, 82nd Airborne Division." I replied, "I was headed to the Alfa Company, 227th Aviation Battalion, First Cavalry Division." I knew Kent had been to jump school because he wore the airborne insignia on his uniform. He had enlisted a year before I got drafted. Kent was not particularly Mr. Army, but he loved adventure. And apparently, he enjoyed jumping out of perfectly good airplanes. Go figure.

Chapter Three

REPORTING FOR DUTY

"Do your duty and leave the rest to heaven."

~ Pierre Corneille

We left Fort Hamilton that afternoon. We traveled by bus to McGuire AFB in New Jersey and flew directly to Killeen, Texas. Killeen was a small Texas town of 50,000 people, mostly active or retired military. It was more like a bedroom community for Fort Hood, probably because Fort Hood is the largest army base in the United States. It is located halfway between Austin and Waco. It is the home of 45,000 soldiers and 8,900 civilian employees. I would come to realize that Fort Hood had a long and rich history. As we landed in Killeen, I could not stop wondering what God had in store for me. But I was glad to have a friend on the journey with me. It almost seemed as if God had orchestrated everything. It was a comforting thought.

Shortly after landing, Kent and I took a taxi to Fort Hood. It was a twenty-minute ride through traffic that reminded me of Los Angeles. As we entered the main gate, I was impressed. Kent and I were about to become part of something bigger than the both of us. Excitement filled the air. Our driver seemed to know exactly where he was going. He took us straight to the receiving center. After several hours of processing, we were officially stationed at Fort Hood. It was time for Kent and me to part ways and report to our separate company headquarters. We made plans to see each other soon, then hugged and said goodbye.

After asking directions to Alfa Company, 227th Aviation Battalion, I started walking. I had to stop three times because of the distance. I was carrying only my duffel bag, but it got heavy real soon. I could have called for an army cab, but I was enjoying looking at the sights. So, after a forty-five-minute walk, I arrived at my new company headquarters. I walked in and reported to the company clerk, who showed me the way to First Sergeant Kirby's office. The First Sergeant wasn't in his office but was expected back any minute. I took a seat outside his door and waited. Moments later, he came walking down the hall.

First Sergeant Kirby was not what I expected. He stood no more than 5 feet 4 inches. My experience with First Sergeants had not been good. When I saw him, I knew he would have a "short-man's attitude." I immediately went on the defensive. As he walked in front of me, he said, "You must be Private Barnett, our new Chaplain's Assistant." His mannerism and tone of voice completely caught me off guard. He was so polite, even respectful. I stood up, and said, "Yes, First Sergeant, Private Barnett reporting for duty." We walked through his door and into the office. He invited me to take a seat, as he walked around to his desk chair. We sat in his office and talked. What was interesting, we talked about all sorts of things. It was like a real conversation, not just army talk. I was completely disarmed.

As I sat there, I wondered if I should mention that I had been AWOL. I would rather have him find out from me than through official channels. So, I took a breath and told him all about my fourteen days of being absent without leave. When I finished, I expected a harsh reaction. What I got, was just the opposite. He looked at me and said, "Private Barnett, I appreciate you telling me, but I already knew. It was in your file, which arrived several days ago." I said, "Oh…um, I didn't realize it would be passed along so fast." He looked at me and said, "As far as I'm concerned, what's in the past is in the past. What I want to know from you is how are you going to proceed from this point?"

I looked at First Sergeant Kirby straight in the eye and said, "I'm going to be the best soldier you have ever seen." He smiled and said, "Great." We continued talking about army life and life particularly at Fort Hood. An hour and half had gone by when the company clerk stuck his head through the door and reminded First Sergeant Kirby, he had a meeting. After getting directions to my barracks, we said goodbye. As I was walking out of the office, First Sergeant Kirby told me not to be late to morning formation. Reveille is at 0700 hours. I smiled and said, "Yes, First Sergeant."

As I left company headquarters, I realized I had just spent almost two hours with the second highest ranking person in my company, after the company commander. This certainly was not basic training or Fort Dix, or even Fort Hamilton. I was not in training anymore. This was my duty station. People seemed more respectful, almost caring. It was a refreshing feeling. It was, however, short lived. When I found my barracks, I was shocked. Up to this point in my military career, I had been assigned to rooms that accommodated two or four individuals. Even during basic training, I only had three other soldiers in my room. Not ideal if you like privacy, but far better than what I was looking at.

My new home was two stories high and as long as a football field. Windows ran down both sides of the building, bottom and top. It was wood framed and painted white, like all the other buildings. I was told later that all the barracks on this side of Fort Hood had been built during WWII. They were due for remodeling, but monies had not been approved by Congress yet. Fort Hood was undergoing a massive face lift, but it was an exceptionally large base and the remodeling was being conducted in stages. As I walked through the front doors, it got even worse. I had been told by the company clerk my bunk assignment was A-28. When I walked inside, I realized there were no individual rooms. It was a wide-open bay with only hanging blankets separating sleeping areas. When I found my assigned sleeping space, I could hardly believe it. A bunk, one footlocker, and no privacy were my new home. I did have a small window above my bunk, something to be grateful for, I guess. There were thirty beds on each side of the room, sixty on the ground floor and sixty on the second floor. Numbers had never been my strongest academic skill, but doing the math in my head, I determined I was living with 119 other soldiers, in a rather intimate way.

There were guys everywhere. Some were playing cards; some were playing checkers or chess. Some were listening to music, actually we were all listening to music. I guess the commissary had run short on headphones. There were at least seven or eight different types of music playing at full volume. I was in hell. I found A-28 and sat on my bunk. I just sat there. I did not know what to do. So much activity and noise, I could not even think. It was early evening on Monday. I was told many of the soldiers in my barracks had just come back from the field after a three-day exercise. They were ready to party. I was ready to sleep. Obviously, that was not going to happen any time soon. I put my stuff in the footlocker, secured it, and went out for a walk.

All of sudden I felt alone. I had not felt like this since my ride with Carol on the San Diego Freeway. I was searching my heart for peace, but I could not find it. How was I going to live in a place like this? Growing up, I did not have brothers or sisters, I was an only child. It had been hard for me to adjust to having roommates, much less an open barracks with 60 strangers. Sure, the blankets provided some privacy, but not much. As I walked along, I started to pray, "Lord, I really need your help. I do not think I can cope with this. Living this way for eighteen more months…I just do not know what to do. Please help me." I walked and prayed for several hours before I went back to the barracks.

When I got back, things had calmed down somewhat. Many of the soldiers had gone out for the evening, probably into Killeen to raise a little hell. There was still music playing, but not as loud. The lights would not go off until 2200 hours. This was going to be a long night. To be at morning formation at 0700 hours, I would need to get up by 0500 hours. I was hoping that two hours would be enough time to hit the mess hall for breakfast and to shave and shower. Fortunately, the latrine would accommodate twenty soldiers at once. As I lay on my bunk, I was still praying silently to myself. I was also remembering my conversation with First Sergeant Kirby. I had felt so good leaving his office. And now, I had no idea how I would get through this.

Sometime during the night, I fell asleep. I had set my alarm for 0500 hours, but it was unnecessary. Except for the soldiers who were on liberty, everyone else was getting up. Alarms were going off everywhere. As I walked to the latrine with twenty of my new friends, I was definitely out of my comfort zone. But I was determined to be a good soldier and I certainly didn't want to be late to formation. I knew First Sergeant Kirby would be looking for me. I showered, then shaved and hurried to the mess hall. I could not eat much because my stomach was unsettled. I finished breakfast and walked back to the barracks for some last-minute fine-tuning of my uniform, then walked to the formation area.

At precisely 0700 hours reveille was played and we all stood at attention in formation. When the flag started up the pole, everyone rendered a salute. Reveille finished, our salutes came down and the morning was under way. First Sergeant Kirby briefed the company on the daily activities, then, we spent thirty minutes doing calisthenics. After our morning exercise, we were dismissed to our duty stations. I had been advised by First Sergeant Kirby the day before to report to the chapel that served our battalion. The company clerk had given me directions. It was a short walk from the barracks, and I was feeling a little better now, but was still worried about my living conditions. I was, however, excited to meet my new chaplain. First Sergeant Kirby had mentioned his name was Chaplain Joe Walker, and then smiled. I was not sure what the smile meant.

After walking about three-quarters of a mile, I turned the corner and saw the chapel. It was beautiful, at least I thought so. It reminded me of an old country church. It was painted white and had a steeple in front. As I looked closer, I could see stained glass windows down the side of the building. Walking toward the chapel, I thought to myself how cool this was. I would be working in a church. I was so excited. Just then something hit me. I could not put my finger on it at first, but something was missing. As I walked up to the front, my eyes were glancing around the property. I did not see a cross. I looked up at the steeple, no cross. I certainly was not an expert on church construction, but every Christian church I could remember had a cross displayed somewhere for people to see. Maybe this was not a church after all.

As I stood in front of the chapel, I knew something was wrong. I kept looking for a cross displayed on or near the building. I stepped back and looked at the steeple one more time just to be sure. I thought to myself, "Yep, no cross up there." I knew I was in the right place. I had followed the company clerk's directions perfectly. I decided to walk in to find answers to my questions. When I entered the front door, I noticed there were two offices on either side. I could not see the plaque on the left side door, but the door on the right said, "Chaplain Eleazar Ari." I did not see anyone in the office, so I continued into the chapel.

Nothing caught my eye right away. There were the stained-glass windows on both sides; pews filled the sanctuary, and a high ceiling above my head. Everything looked normal. I could tell it was an old building, but with amazing character. Still walking, I turned around and looked up toward the rear and saw what appeared to be a choir loft. The woodwork was beautiful. Half-way into the sanctuary, I focused on the front and stopped in my tracks. There was no cross because this was a Jewish Synagogue.

Fort Hood, TX 1972

It took a few seconds for my mind to register what I was seeing. There was an altar and on top of it was a large scroll. I could see two handles and partly unrolled paper. I remember watching the *Ten Commandments* with Charlton Heston playing Moses. It looked like a scene from the movie. Behind the altar was a large piece of red fabric hanging from the ceiling to the floor. Just in front of the fabric was a hanging light. It looked like a chandelier that would hang over the dining table, but smaller. It was gold and had a light flickering inside the glass. It did not flicker like a candle, so I figured it must be electrical. It was ornate and lovely.

Standing there, trying to take everything in, I heard a voice call out, "Can I help you?" I turned around and saw a figure standing near the front doors. The doors were glass, so the light behind the figure prevented me from seeing clearly. I started to walk toward the person and said, "Yes, I hope so. My name is Private Terry Barnett and I am the new Chaplain's Assistant for the 227th Aviation Battalion. I am looking for Chaplain Joe Walker. I was told he had an office in this chapel." As I got closer, I saw a hand come toward me and heard, "Hey, nice to meet you. I am Michael Goldstein, Chaplain Ari's assistant. Call me Mike."

I reached out and shook Mike's hand. He seemed like a friendly lad. He stood about 5 feet 6 inches and looked too young to be in the army, much less a Private First Class. His face was cheerful, freckled, and he had the whitest teeth I had ever seen. Maybe that is why he smiled so much. As we talked, he seemed happy I was there. He told me about what it had been like working for Chaplain Ari. He mentioned he did not know Chaplain Walker very well, but that he seemed like a nice guy. On Tuesdays, there was an all post chaplains' meeting that usually lasted most of the day. "You probably won't meet Chaplain Walker today," he said, smiling.

We talked through the morning, went to lunch, and came back to finish out the day. Mike gave me a tour of the chapel that was now a synagogue. He had told me that ordinary army chapels were designed to accommodate three faiths: Christian, Catholic, and Jewish. However, since there was a high percentage of Jewish personal at Fort Hood, the army had decided to designate this chapel exclusively for Jewish worshippers. Mike went on to say that Chaplain Walker and his assistant had offices in the building. Apparently, having office space near the men and women of the 227th was to give them easier access to pastoral care and counseling.

My first day as a Chaplain's Assistant had been far from what I had expected; I had yet to meet my new chaplain and I would be working in a Jewish synagogue. Who would have imagined? During our conversation, Mike told me he would be leaving within the month. His enlistment was up, and he was planning to open a restaurant in New York City. Raised in an orthodox home, Mike described himself as a secular Jew. He celebrated the high holy days of the Jewish faith, but with no real conviction.

Lying in my semi-private bunk that evening, I thought about my conversation with Mike. Although I did not know him well, I felt sorry for him. He was part of God's chosen people, but only knew God in academic terms. I felt led to pray for him. I reached over to the small nightstand that was beside my bunk, opened the metal drawer and removed two ear plugs. Placing the plugs in my ears lowered the noise level to a hushed roar. Lights would go off soon and hopefully the music would as well. Drifting off, I prayed for Mike.

Next morning was much like the one before. I woke up at 0530 hours, made a dash to the latrine, then off to the mess hall, made morning formation, and was off to my new office. I could not get over that I was working in a synagogue and not a church. God must have an interesting sense of humor, I thought. Walking to the synagogue, I was hoping that Chaplain Walker would be there; I was anxious to meet him. I arrived a few minutes before 0800 hours. As I walked in, I was greeted with, "You must be Private Barnett, my new assistant. I'm Joe Walker." "Yes sir, I am," I replied as we shook hands. "I'm glad to finally meet you Chaplain Walker."

Now I know why First Sergeant Kirby was smiling when he told me Chaplain Walker's name. Chaplain Walker was not an ordinary chaplain. Most chaplains enlist in the army after seminary. They want to serve God and the military. Chaplain Walker had been a decorated infantry captain and an army ranger prior to becoming a chaplain. He served two tours in Vietnam, then came back and attended seminary. As we sat in his office, I continued to ask questions about his army career and faith journey. It was impressive. As we talked, I had a sense that Chaplain Walker was a godly man. He struck me as a man that had made peace with himself and God, probably not an easy thing after Vietnam.

Here was a man who stood 6 feet 2 inches, no visible body fat, had commanded soldiers for twelve years, and was an airborne ranger.

Now he is a chaplain and a follower of Jesus Christ. Wow! I knew right then; this man would have a significant impact on my life. As we talked, the conversation came easy. Besides being easy to talk with, Chaplain Walker's eyes had a sparkle. Telling him about my brief faith journey is when I noticed his eyes. He was genuinely interested in my story and we talked for about an hour before we decided there was work to do.

I was getting settled in my office when Mike came in. He wanted to know if I would like to have lunch with him and Chaplain Ari. After checking with Chaplain Walker, I told Mike I would love to. I was excited about meeting a Jewish rabbi. In my twenty years, I had never met a rabbi. I knew truly little about the Old Testament and Jewish history, so I was looking forward to meeting Chaplain Ari. I assumed we would have lunch in the mess hall or some restaurant on base. As I was preparing to break for lunch, Mike came into my office. "Hey Terry, are you ready?" he asked, smiling. "Yes." I said with anticipation. "Great, I'll meet you in the kitchen," Mike replied.

The kitchen was in the southwest corner of the synagogue. I had walked through it several times the day before. It had all the usual appliances. There was a stove, refrigerator, sink, and a small table. It was clean and had a nice view of Darnell Medical Center. As we walked towards the kitchen, I asked Mike, "Why the kitchen, I thought we were going out?" Mike replied with one word, "Kosher." I said, "Kosher…um, what's kosher?" "You'll find out," he said with a grin. We walked into the kitchen, and there stood a young man with a funny round, flat hat on his head. It looked like a small saucer. He did not appear to be much older than me.

As we entered, Chaplain Ari turned around, "Ah, you must be Chaplain Walker's new assistant, shalom my friend," he said with a smile. "Yes, I am, it is nice to meet you sir. My name is Private Terry Barnett," I said. Chaplain Ari had prepared lunch for us. We sat at the small table and enjoyed a delightful time. I experienced the same relaxed feelings I had with Chaplain Walker. All chaplains are commissioned officers, holding the rank of captain or above. Noncommissioned officers or enlisted personnel, such as me, generally treat commissioned officers with the utmost respect. Conversations are formal with "yes sir or no sir."

I did not want to ask too many questions and look stupid. I did finally ask Chaplain Ari about our lunch, which was incredibly good. There were, however, smells and textures I was unfamiliar with. When I asked the question, Chaplain Ari's face beamed like a light from a lighthouse. "Well, Terry, you are eating a traditional Jewish meal," he replied. First, he explained what kosher meant. Then, with pride in his voice, Chaplain Ari walked me through our lunch.

It was a three-course meal. Chaplain Ari described the first dish as matzah ball soup. It was a type of dumpling. There were quarter-size bread balls. Some were heavier than others and sank in the bowl, while others floated at the top. Chaplain Air called them, "Floaters and sinkers," almost giggling. The floaters and sinkers seemed to be dancing as they moved in the chicken broth with carrots and celery. We also had blintzes or crepes. This was my favorite part of the meal. Chaplain Ari described blintzes as thin, flat pancakes rolled around a filling. He had prepared ours with an apple and blueberry filling. They looked like an egg roll and were served with applesauce. Really good. Chaplain Ari continued to smile and beam as he described the next course. It was called holishkes or stuffed cabbage. Cabbage leaves stuffed with meatballs in a tomato-based, sweet-and-sour sauce. It was my first Jewish meal and it was delicious. The smells of the different spices were captivating.

As our lunch was coming to an end, I was dying to ask Chaplain Ari about his little hat. But I could not find the courage. I certainly did not want to be disrespectful. Just like with Chaplain Walker the day before, my first encounter with Chaplain Ari had been delightful. He was informative, gracious, and very orthodox in his practice of

Judaism.   Once again, I was sure I would learn much from this gentleman. I thanked him for our lunch and returned to my office. The rest of my day consisted of typing letters for Chaplain Walker and filing. It was a good day. I wish I could say the same for the nights. As my workday ended, I was tired, but in a good way.

I was facing another night in the barracks or as I like to call it, "The hell hole." This would be my third night and I just could not imagine living there another fourteen months. I left the office and went to the mess hall. Army food was not an experience you looked forward to, but it was filling. I finished dinner and walked to the "hell hole." As I walked in the front doors, I smelled a strange odor, like burning rope. Then it hit me, marijuana. Great. I'm surrounded by a bunch of potheads. This just gets better and better I mumble to myself. I walked to my blanket secured bedroom and changed. I placed my uniform on a hanger and hung it on a hook near my bed. Then slipped on a pair of sweats and laid on my bunk. Depressed.

As I lay there, my mind drifted back to San Diego and surfing. I missed it. I was enjoying my work and the sense of accomplishment, but I also missed my freedom and the ocean. The ocean was my freedom. I felt most alive when sliding down the face of a six-foot wave. The feeling of speed and power and control was intoxicating, even addictive. The surfing lifestyle had been my identity. But suddenly I was reminded in my spirit, I had a new identity. My new identity was in Christ. I still missed surfing, but I was comforted by the truth that God loved me, and my sins had been forgiven. It brought me peace.

I reached under my pillow and pulled out my Bible. I was flipping through the pages and my eyes landed on 2 Corinthians 1:4, *"…the God of all comfort, who comforts us in all our troubles…"* I read this over and over. I knew this comfort, and I was grateful for it. As I lay there, I started to pray that God would give me strength to endure my living conditions. I felt like I was surrounded by the enemy. I was in hostile territory, both physically and spiritually. I reminded myself how faithful God had been. From the moment I accepted Christ as my Lord while being AWOL until now, He had been faithful. I did not know how He would do it, but I knew He would work this out…this "hell hole."

Lights went out at 2200 hours and I started to drift off. I was sure tomorrow would be another eventful day. I was just about asleep when a question ran through my mind. Where was Mike Goldstein? In the three days I had been here I had not seen him in the barracks. Being assigned to the same workstation, we should be living in the same place. It seemed odd I had not come across him here. Maybe he lived upstairs, and I just had not seen him. I will ask him tomorrow, I thought to myself. Then in a quiet moment, my thoughts faded into dreams.

Chapter Four

FINDING GOD'S FINGERPRINTS
IN HARD TIMES

"A diamond is a chunk of coal that did well under pressure."

~ Henry Kissinger

I arrived at my office before 0740 hours. As I unlocked the front doors and walked in, I noticed Mike was already in his office. I stopped in his doorway, "Boy, Mike," I said with a smile, "you must live here." He gave me an inquisitive look and replied, "Well…you know…um, how did you know?" I was about to walk away until I heard his words. I stopped and poked my head back in his office and said, "You're kidding me, right? You actually live here…in the chapel, I mean synagogue?" Mike looked at me with a twinge of horror and tried to speak, "I couldn't - wouldn't, I mean, who would – ever consider doing that?"

As I looked at him with a raised eyebrow, his shoulders drooped with an embarrassing smirk growing across his face, and I knew, Mike was living in the synagogue. That is the reason I had never seen him in the barracks. "Okay, I am," he said with a slight sneer, "but you can't tell anyone." I raised my hand and crossed my heart, saying, "I promise." Mike got up from his desk and said, "Come on…" I followed him up the stairs to the choir loft. At the top of the stairs there was a door. He opened the door, and we walked into an open room overlooking the entire room below. It felt like being in a balcony of a theater.

As I looked over the three-foot high railing, I could see the altar area, the door to my office and to the kitchen. Most of the pews were visible as were the stained-glass windows. Standing at the front railing, I noticed a three-foot walkway running the length of the room. Then the floor raised six inches with a six-foot flat surface, and then raised again, six inches. There were three raised sections towards the back wall. I assumed this floor construction was for the choir, so people behind were raised and able to see. In a Jewish synagogue, however, there was no choir. Mike had moved a bunk into the loft and placed it on the first raised section. From the ground floor it was not visible. What an ingenious move on Mike's part, I thought.

We were standing near Mike's bunk as he explained to me how he managed to pull this off. He said with a smile, "It wasn't hard. I have a friend in supply and asked him if he had a spare bunk in the warehouse." He continued with a sense of pride, "My friend dropped the bunk off, and I put it up here, because no one ever comes up here." Mike went on to explain how he uses the barracks latrine to clean up and always makes morning formation. He was not sure if First Sergeant Kirby knew he slept up here, but he was not going to ask.

Later that day it struck me; Mike had mentioned when we first met that his enlistment was up at the end of the month. In twenty-one days, he would no longer be living in the choir loft, but I would be. I spent the next three weeks preparing to move. And move I did. On Mike's last day, I spent my first night sleeping in a Jewish synagogue. It was so quiet it was a bit eerier. I did not sleep well, but I was sure I would get used to it. I had my stereo with headphones, music, and all my personal stuff, so I was content. I made sure I was up every morning in time to clean up and make formation. I had my uniforms pressed and starched every week. I looked and acted as a committed soldier.

Over the next six months I was promoted twice, from a private [E-1] to private first class [E-3] and was a model soldier. I took over the administrative duties for Chaplain Ari. The army had refused to provide him with another full-time assistant because he was leaving the army. It made for long days and many weekends of work, but I did not mind. I was working for two amazing chaplains. Chaplain Ari taught me about the Old Testament from a Jewish perspective; Chaplain Walker showed me how to follow Jesus from the heart.

I had only seen my friend, Kent Stacy twice in six months. His life was much different than mine. He was a Chaplains' Assistant, but he was assigned to an airborne unit. He was always in the field, training. His chaplain was assigned to the First Air Cavalry, which was a part of a combat aviation brigade. The whole purpose of the air cavalry was air assault. Air assault is the movement of ground-based military forces by vertical take-off and landing (VTOL) aircraft—such as the helicopter—to seize and hold key terrain which has not been fully secured, and to directly engage enemy forces. In addition to regular infantry training, air-assault units receive training in rappelling, air transportation, and jumping from Huey helicopters.

My unit was also aviation, but we held a support role rather than a direct combat role. Most of my work was administrative and helping Chaplain Walker on Sundays with services. Hearing how much time Kent spent in the field, training, I was grateful for my job. That was about to change, however. I had received word that the entire Frist Cavalry Battalion was going to hold a joint two-week field exercise. I was excited about seeing my friend, Kent, but I was far less excited about two weeks in the field. Sleeping in tents, eating field rations from plastic bags, and playing combat was not my idea of fun.

The day arrived for Chaplain Walker and me to join the other chaplains and assistants for a briefing about the field exercise. It would be an all-day affair. Kent and I sat together. He took this much more seriously than I did. There was a good reason for that, he would be yelling, "Ranger, hooah," as he jumped out of helicopters risking his life. I, on the other hand, planned to stay on the ground and help serve communion to the troops. I would be thinking, this is the Lord's body broken for you, hooah.

The following day, I went to the motor pool to sign-out a jeep for Chaplain Walker and me. This would be our transportation for the next two weeks. It was 0930 hours when we left the synagogue and drove to the main staging area for the exercise. Since this operation involved the whole First Cavalry Battalion it was huge. There were nine companies, consisting of 2,100 soldiers conducting war games. It was impressive. The field command center with its strategic operations was a tent the size of a football field. There were a hundred men and women scurrying around, from generals to privates, trying to keep the operation on track. It was no small task.

My unit had been assigned to support Kent's airborne unit. It would be my pilots and crew from the 227th that would be flying Kent and his commando types around the theater of operation. Chaplains go wherever the troops go. When they go into combat, chaplains and their assistants go too. In a combat situation, the primary duty of the assistant is to protect the chaplain. Chaplains do not carry weapons, their assistants do. Like Chaplain Walker, Kent's chaplain was an airborne ranger. The difference was that Chaplain Walker was assigned to a support unit and not a combat unit. Every time I thought about it, all I could say was, "Thank you, God."

The "games," as I called them went along reasonably well. There were some minor injuries within our unit, but nothing serious. There were, however, numerous inherent dangers with an operation of this size. With maneuvers going 24/7, helicopters flying around the clock, and everyone exhausted, accidents are likely. The theater of operation was a twenty-five square mile area. The terrain in Central Texas is flat with an occasional hill, but we had been instructed to imagine the terrain in Vietnam as we played our "games."

I was not sure what command meant by "imagine." It was impossible for me to imagine Vietnam since I had never been there. But these were only pretend games, so I guess command thought we could pretend Vietnam as well. It was the second week of pretending when things went horribly wrong. Chaplain Walker and I were hitching a ride with Kent and his chaplain. The pilot of the Huey was transporting us to our company. We had been at the command center all day. Kent and his chaplain would be jumping from 10,000 feet with several others. They were on duty this evening, practicing night ranger training.

It was dark, so the pilot was flying by instruments. The rangers would jump, and Chaplain Walker and I would fly on to our unit. I was a wreck. It was exciting to fly, but the thought of jumping into the night left my mouth spit-less. Kent, on the other hand, was grinning like a kid in a candy store. From my perspective, he had a few screws loose. I had to keep reminding myself; rangers do this all the time, that is why there are rangers. As we approached the drop zone, the pilot gave the five-minute warning. The six rangers checked each other's gear and gave thumbs up. They were ready.

As Chaplain Walker and I moved out of the way, three rangers went to the port side and three to the starboard side of the helicopter. They would free fall for twenty seconds then pull their chutes. This would give them enough time to clear each other as they left the helicopter. All six rangers were wearing night vision goggles. I had talked with Kent before takeoff about this training exercise and he said, "You know Terry, I love jumping, but night jumps are always scary. There are so many things that can go wrong." I asked him if he was having a bad feeling about this exercise, he replied, "No, not really…you know…um, maybe a little."

As the six rangers stood in the doorway of the Huey, I knew Kent was nervous. I had only known Kent since Chaplain Assistants' school, but I had never seen him so concerned. Besides our conversation prior to take off, I could see it in his eyes. Kent was the strongest Christian I knew. His walk with the Lord had always inspired me. Through my helmet, I heard the one-minute warning from the pilot. Kent glanced back at me and smiled, and then gave a thumbs up. I did the same to him. Then I heard the pilot say, "Ten seconds…nine, eight…go!" All six rangers left the helicopter at the same moment. I moved to the port side where Kent had been. I watched him fall away into the night.

The pilot banked left and flew west. It was beautiful; the sun had been down for forty-five minutes, leaving a lingering beauty that was breathtaking. It was an amazing sight with the reds and oranges fading into the florescent blue as twilight disappeared, leaving only stars. As I was looking out the doorway, Chaplain Walker said, "So what do you think?" "It's beautiful," I replied. "Yes, it is, but I was talking about something else," he said with a grin. "What were you referring to, sir?" I said. His grin got wider, and he said, "Do you want to learn to jump?" Now I had a grin and calmly said, "Ugh, absolutely not, but thanks for asking."

For the next five minutes we sat in silence, enjoying the beauty of God's creation. As we were making our approach to land, the radio came alive. I could hear intense chatter, but had difficulty making it out. As I strained to listen, I heard the words "accident" and "rangers." Then I remembered what Kent had said about his feelings. I knew something was wrong, very wrong. I kept listening to my radio for any hint of the problem. Our pilot came on the radio and said, "Chaplain Walker, Sir, I have orders to turn around and go back to the drop zone. There's been an accident involving three of the rangers." Chaplain Walker replied, "Of course."

We turned and headed back. It was a fifteen-minute flight. Our pilot was monitoring radio channels that Chaplain Walker and I did not have access to. Half-way back to the drop zone, the pilot advised Chaplain Waker that three of the rangers had become entangled. Apparently, their parachutes became twisted and failed to open. My mind was running wild. Was Kent one of them? How bad was it? Was anyone dead? Chaplain Walker asked me, "Are you all right?" I must have had a panicked look on my face because he asked me again, "Are you all right?" As I stared at him, I managed to say, "Um…yea, I think so. I'm worried about Kent." He reached over and grabbed my shoulder, then said, "Let's pray."

As we approached the drop zone, I could see bright lights flashing. In the distance, I could see more on the way. My heart was racing. I had never experienced anything like this before. It seemed like a lot of activity for a parachuting accident. Then I saw the downed helicopter. As we got closer, I realized there was wreckage everywhere. People were scrambling in every direction. Three ambulances had arrived, and eight paramedics were rushing to attend the injured. As our helicopter touched down, Chaplain Walker immediately jumped out and ran towards a person sitting under a large oak tree. He was bleeding badly from his forehead. I would find out later he was Specialist Fourth Class Jason Ray, crew chief on the helicopter that was now in pieces.

The main debris field was extensive. There were burning pieces of helicopter everywhere. The fuselage was upside down and partly hanging in a tree. Through the smoke I could see one of the pilots still inside. He was not moving. The paramedics were working frantically to remove him. There was a body lying on the ground ten yards away. His face had been covered with a flight jacket and I presumed this was the other pilot. Chaplain Walker was talking with one of the paramedics when a loud explosion pierced the night air. Part of the tail section exploded and sent pieces of helicopter everywhere.

As I stood looking at this chaotic scene, it felt surreal. When the paramedics removed the pilot, they placed him on a stretcher. As they walked in front of me, I noticed the pilot was missing his left arm and part of his right leg. A nauseous wave of pain broke over me. I turned away from the wreckage and vomited. Moments later, I felt a hand on my shoulder. Chaplain Walker was standing behind me. He asked me if I was going to be okay, and I responded, "Yes sir, I think so." He helped me to stand and asked if I had seen Chaplain Johnson and the rangers who had jumped from our helicopter. I said, "No, I haven't…" I immediately thought of Kent and felt another wave of vomiting overtake me. This time I fought it back and started to scan the area for my friend.

It felt like I had been watching this scene for an hour, but when I glanced at my watch, I realized it had been barely five minutes. I heard sirens in the distance and moments later four Fort Hood fire trucks were on the scene. As the fire fighters started their battle with the burning debris and fuel spills, I had a strange thought: this could be a movie scene. But it wasn't a movie, it was real. Somewhere, in the darkness was Kent. Was he alive? Was he dead? I had no idea.

I did not have a flashlight, so searching far from the crash site was difficult. As I was walking around, I was yelling, "Kent…Chaplain Johnson… Kent…" This went on for a few minutes when I heard, "Over here. We're over here." I turned and looked in the direction of the voices and saw a group walking towards me from the woods. I ran in their direction, yelling to the paramedics who were standing nearby. Chaplain Walker heard me yelling and came running. The six rangers who had jumped from our helicopter were alive.

Kent and Chaplain Johnson were carrying one of the rangers on a makeshift stretcher. The other two rangers were helping a second injured ranger to walk. Both injured men had broken bones, but no life-threatening injuries. I looked at Kent and smiled. Looking strained, he flashed me a grin and said, "What took you so long?" I did not know if he was making a joke or whether he was serious. With a serious look, I said, "Kent, we lost two pilots." I knew rangers were trained to deal with extreme events, but I was not. I did not know how to process the events around me. When Kent heard that two pilots had died, his expression changed. He said, "Oh, Terry, I'm sorry. I didn't know."

I sat with Kent in the ambulance as the paramedics were checking him out. He told me what had happened after they jumped. Kent described the exit from the helicopter and the twenty- second free fall as normal. "Everything was going fine", Kent said. They all pulled their parachutes according to plan, then, about three minutes into the descent another helicopter came out of nowhere. Kent continued, "We could hear it coming, but couldn't see it." Apparently, there had been an electrical malfunction and all the lights were out on the aircraft. Since this was a combat simulated jump, the rangers had no visible lighting.

"We could hear the helicopter's approach, but still didn't see anything," Kent said. As I listened to his story, I was speechless. He went on about the sound of the helicopter's rotor blades and the boom they make with every rotation. The sound was getting closer and closer. Kent decided to light a flair stick so their position would be visible and with the illumination of the flair, the sky lit up. The approaching helicopter was within a hundred feet when it veered hard to starboard attempting to miss the rangers.

When the helicopter turned, the wind from the rotor blades pushed two of the rangers together tangling their parachutes. When they tangled, the parachutes collapsed, and both rangers started to free fall. "By some miracle," Kent said with a wink," both men fell into a reservoir filled with water. They hit hard, and sustained some serious broken bones, but they were alive," Kent continued "We were humping back to our rendezvous point when I heard you calling. We knew the pilots had lost control of the helicopter but hadn't seen where they landed."

Sitting in the ambulance listening to Kent tell the story, I noticed he was much more serious. The death of the two pilots had shaken him too. Missions going wrong, broken bones, and carrying guys out of the bush was all part of an army ranger's life. But death is always hard, even for the most hardened soldier. We did not know exactly what had happened. There would be an official investigation by the army and the FAA. In the coming days, every aspect of Kent's mission would be scrutinized. A lot of people would be asking a lot of questions. Why was a helicopter flying where rangers were conducting airborne operations? Why was the helicopter flying without any running lights? Why couldn't the pilots recover the aircraft after veering off? Was it human error or mechanical error or both? There were so many questions.

The paramedics finished the field examination on Kent and the other rangers. They would be taken to the Darnell Army Medical Center on Fort Hood for follow-up. As I watched the ambulance pull away, Chaplain Walker walked over and said, "We are about done here. Are you ready to go? We have been requested to return to command for a debriefing." I said, "Yes…yes, I'm ready. This is going to be a long night isn't it?" He replied, "Yes, Terry it will be."

The next day I went to the hospital to see Kent. He was doing fine, but hospital staff had wanted to keep him twenty-four hours for observation. He was scheduled to leave that afternoon and was anxious to get back to his unit. The camaraderie that Kent enjoyed with his ranger buddies was impressive. They were a tight-knit group; they lived together; they trained together; and they would die together if necessary. I told Kent about the debriefing that Chaplain Walker and I had gone through. The preliminary finding was the rangers had not contributed to the accident. Kent was relieved to hear the news.

Chaplain Walker and I finished our time in the field without any further problems. We held three worship services on Sunday, the last day of the "games." Because of the extended time in the field and the accident, Chaplain Walker gave me a few days off. I drove down to Galveston and walked along the beach. I even rented a surfboard and went surfing. Three glorious days in the sun and I was a new man. The following Monday I was back in the office ready to go.

The next several months flew by as they often do when you are busy. In the army, time seems to pass differently than in civilian life. The rhythm of army life revolves around duty and assignments. There are times when you work two or three weeks straight, then, take some extended time off. Completion of the assignment is the guiding force. I had two and one-half months left in the army and was up for another promotion. This promotion involved being interviewed by a three-person board. My first three promotions were automatic with good performance reviews. If promoted, I would go from Private First Class to Specialist Fourth Class, (SP-4) and a considerable jump in pay.

My interview board was in two weeks and I wanted to do well. I wanted this promotion because it would mean I had served my country with honor. I would like to leave the army in a far different way than I had entered the army. Chaplain Walker told me he would be part of the interview process. He and two other individuals would be asking me questions about my job, army protocol, and future-plans regarding the army. I felt certain I could answer the first two, but I was not planning to re-enlist. I wondered if that would destroy my chances for the promotion.

On the day of my interview I was nervous. It was set for 1530 hours, so I had the morning and part of the afternoon to finish preparing. I had been re-reading material from my class at Chaplain Assistants' school and army protocol manuals. I felt prepared except for the career question. If they asked me if I planned to stay in the army, I would tell them no. I was sure Chaplain Walker would go easy on me; the other two individuals, I wasn't sure.

The day progressed as usual. I studied, did clerical work, and went to lunch. After lunch I went back to my office and spent some time in prayer. My interview was at battalion headquarters and I did not want to be late. I wore my dress greens which are like a suit in the military. I had gotten a haircut the day before, so I felt ready. There was a saying I picked up somewhere, "Look sharp, be sharp." I drove to headquarters and met Chaplain Walker in the foyer. He gave me a few words of encouragement before we walked into the conference room.

It was an impressive room, with mahogany walls and large bay windows that overlooked an athletic field. It was on this field where Fort Hood conducted its military ceremonies. As I walked in, I saw First Sergeant Kirby and another first sergeant I did not recognize. Chaplain Walker walked around the conference table and joined the other two men. We sat down across from each other and I knew I was in the hot seat. Chaplain Walker started the interview by asking me to state my name, rank, and position. I responded, "Terry W. Barnett, Private First Class, Chaplain's Assistant to Chaplain Joe Walker."

The interview seemed to go well. I had done my homework and felt I answered all the questions to the board's satisfaction. At least I felt that until the last question. As the interview was coming to a close, First Sergeant Kirby asked me if I planned to reenlist and remain in the army. I took a breath and looked him in the eye and said, "First Sergeant, I do not plan to reenlist, but I would like very much to leave the army with integrity and honor. I had a rough start, as you know, but I hope to finish well. That's why this promotion is important to me." First Sergeant Kirby wrote a note on a pad, then looked at Chaplain Walker and said, "Sir, I have no additional questions for Private Barnett." The chaplain asked, "Private Barnett, would you like to add anything?" I said, "No, sir."

I stood and thanked the panel for their time and left the room. As I was driving back to my office, I was not feeling as confident as I had earlier. I was sure the last question had sunk me. It would take a week for me to hear about my promotion. Regardless of whether I got promoted, I had only two and half months left in the army and needed to start thinking about my civilian career. I had no idea what I would do after the army. I knew this needed to be a point of prayer. God had been so faithful throughout my army enlistment. I was confident He would not abandon me in my civilian life.

As I got closer to leaving the army, time seemed to slow down. Waiting to hear about my promotion felt like a month rather than a week. It was midweek and movie night for my company. I seldom went to movie night because I attended a Bible study on Wednesday nights. This week, however, I had decided to go with some friends. My Bible study had concluded the week previously, and I had a free night. I had no idea that this Wednesday night would put me on a course that would change my life.

The day started normal enough. I rolled out of my bunk, walked to my barracks to clean up, then to the mess hall. I was back at work by 0745 hours. Chaplain Walker would arrive after lunch. He had an officer's meeting the third Wednesday of every month. I could have slept-in and gotten away with it, but I had always been an early riser. In the sixteen months I had been at Fort Hood, I had only missed one morning formation. There was a flu bug going around the base and I became a host. I was sick for a week. I felt so bad; I thought I might not live through it. Actually, I was not that sick, but it was troubling.

When Chaplain Walker arrived, we had an hour meeting about Sundays. He was making some changes in the worship format and wanted my opinion. I appreciated that about him. Even though he was a strong leader, he always wanted to hear the thoughts and opinions of others. We talked about the Sunday format, and then he gave me six letters to type. I made several follow-up phone calls for him and the workday was done. I needed to be at the theater by 1900 hours to meet my friends. The movie started at 1930 hours. After work I went to the mess hall then to my barracks to freshen up.

When I arrived at the theater, two of my friends were standing outside. I did not know prior to arriving, but we were seeing Serpico. Al Pacino stars as Frank Serpico, the New York City police officer that exposed corruption within the police department. I was mesmerized by the film. I went back three more times to see it. There was a significant amount of profanity, which I did not care for, but the story was captivating. Serpico's sense of purpose and integrity was compelling. After seeing the movie and reading the book I knew what I wanted to do after the army.

The following week I received word about my promotion. Walking into the office after morning formation I noticed Chaplain Walker was already in his office. As I passed his door, he looked up and smiled. I returned the smile and said, "Good morning sir." He replied, "Good morning Specialist Barnett." I abruptly stopped and whirled around. Walking into his office, I said, "What did you say, sir?" Chaplain Walker smiled again and said, "Good morning Specialist." He handed me an envelope that looked official. I opened it and read the letter in front of Chaplain Walker.

I was holding in my hand orders promoting me to Specialist Fourth Class. I think Chaplain Walker was as excited as I was. He stood up and shook my hand and congratulated me. He asked me to sit down, so I took a seat. The way he scooted his chair around, I could tell he had something he wanted to say. He looked at me with a serious expression and said, "Terry, I'm going to tell you something that you cannot repeat. If you do, and it gets back to my supervisor, I would be in trouble." I said with an inquisitive look," Absolutely sir, my lips are sealed."

Chaplain Walker leaned towards me as if someone might be listening, and said, "What your orders don't tell is your overall score." He went on to talk about how the accumulated score involves interview presentation, work performance, and overall soldiering. Then he said, my overall score was the second highest he had ever seen. I could not believe it. I asked him how that could be. He said, my sincerity and speaking from the heart was appreciated by the board. I thanked him for telling me and then wondered why he did. Maybe he was hoping I would reenlist. Whatever the reason, it was nice to know.

It had been three weeks since the crash and the army released its findings to the command staff. It would be another week before it went public. Chaplain Walker received the report and shared the highlights with me. The investigation revealed the crash was caused by a combination of pilot error and electrical malfunction. When the pilot realized he was about to fly into the paratroopers, he over corrected the aircraft into a downward dive. This maneuver caused the aircraft to stall which was unrecoverable. The lack of illumination of the aircraft resulted in the ranger's inability to signal their location in a timely manner. The report concluded the six rangers were not at fault.

I was relieved to hear the final report. I know Kent had several sleepless nights wondering about the outcome. As Chaplain Walker was telling me about the report, he also mentioned that the crew chief would make a full recovery. The most interesting aspect of the final report was the language used to explain pilot error. The report called both pilots "heroic" even though they were partly the cause. The evasive maneuver that ultimately placed the aircraft into the dive saved the lives of six men. The army would close the case highlighting this fact, rather than pilot error.

My time in the army was coming to an end. My original exit date was June 20, 1974, but I would need to make up the fourteen days I lost during my AWOL experience. My new exit date was July 7, 1974. Living in the synagogue had been an extraordinary experience. I was able to have privacy and enjoy quiet time in the evenings. Chaplain Walker had a major influence on my life. His sense of duty and love for Christ was inspiring. We had decided to meet in Colorado and do some mountain climbing after my enlistment was up. I was looking forward to spending time with him that was not army related.

During my last week at Fort Hood, most of my time was spent getting ready to transition to civilian life. The army kept trying to convince me to reenlist, but I held to my guns. I was determined to get out and start a career in law enforcement. I had a strong desire to protect the unprotected and right every wrong. I know that sounds idealistic, but I was determined to change the world. In many ways, I had come into the army a boy, but I was leaving a man. I had a few obstacles in front of me before I could achieve my goal, but nothing was going to stand in my way.

My last weekend in the synagogue was uneventful. I would be leaving Fort Hood on Monday and I was feeling nostalgic. I had lived in a Jewish synagogue for almost sixteen months. It was my home. I was going to miss it. But I was excited about how God was going to lead me in civilian life. Over the weekend I thought about what God had in store for me. Sunday night a verse in Jeremiah 29 kept running through my mind, *"I know the plans I have for you," says the Lord. "They are plans for good and not disaster, to give you a future and a hope"* [29:11]. This brought me a lot of reassurance that God had a plan for my life. I went to sleep thanking God.

Monday morning, I woke-up early. The clock read 0430 hours. Uncharacteristic for me, I was wide awake. I had an appointment with the company clerk and First Sergeant Kirby at 0900 hours to begin processing out. I had been informed it should only take couple of hours to complete the processing. I would be on the road by noon, driving to Colorado. I was planning to spend several days with Chaplain Walker, who flew out on Friday to visit family in Denver. I was driving and figured two days to make the drive.

Chaplain Walker's parents lived outside Denver. They were elderly and he had wanted to see them for some time. Before he left Fort

Hood, we decided to meet and spend a day climbing Mount Evans, which rises 14,240 feet into the air. It was a beautiful mountain. The climbing is moderate and took us twelve hours to make the round trip. I spent the night with Chaplain Walker and left for California the next morning. I would never see him again, but he remained in my heart.

I returned to Bakersfield, California where I had grown up and started working on my civilian career. Ever since I saw the movie Serpico on that Wednesday night in the army, I had wanted to be a police officer. I was twenty-two years old and full of determination. I enrolled at Bakersfield Junior College to study Criminal Justice.

Up to this point in my life, the only academic success I had achieved was Chaplains' Assistant school. I had started Mesa Junior College in San Diego prior to getting drafted, but surfing got in the way. I had morning classes and the surf is always the best in the mornings. That created an inherent conflict and surfing always took precedence. Because of my priorities at the time, I was unable to keep up with the demands of college, so I dropped out. This time I knew it would be different. I was motivated and confident that I could be successful.

In addition to working on an associate degree, I applied and was accepted to the Kern County Sheriff's Academy. This was a twelve-month program to train reserve deputies for patrol duties. It was a demanding training experience, but I excelled and was grateful to God and my parents for their support. Graduating after twelve months was one of the happiest days of my life.

As I looked back over my army experience and first year of civilian life, I marvel at how God had worked. The journey of faith and trust in Jesus Christ had changed my life forever. And then I realized, the journey had just begun.

His fingerprints continue…

Graduation Day with Parents (Rae Dixon and Pete Barnett) 1975
Graduation from Kern County Sheriff's Dept., Reserve Class

Part Two

Chapter Five

DEATH, THE FINAL FRONTIER

"Death is not the opposite of life, but a part of it."

~ Haruki Murakami

Facing Death with No Regrets

When I first decided to write a book on death and dying, I was overwhelmed with the prospect. I was convinced however, that what I had discovered in my doctorate research was important and people needed to hear it. With over twenty years of helping people to die well I have learned that death does not come easily. Let me explain what I mean by dying well. Dying well involves a sense of peace about the inevitable transition. For most people, however, peace is elusive. One or more areas of their lives do not have closure and therefore they are not ready to transition. This spiritual, mental, and/or emotional state results in feelings of disconnection and apprehension.

Every human being has a story. Our lives are made up of hundreds and hundreds of short stories. There is a beginning and an end with hundreds of stories making chapters that tell about our life journey. There are wonderful chapters and there are difficult chapters. When these chapters are put together, they define our lives; explain our lives. Some chapters are even celebrated. The birth of a child, each birthday thereafter, graduations, weddings, anniversaries are just a few that we celebrate. These are chapters of our lives. We even celebrate the dead. We hold funerals and memorial services to celebrate a life after someone has passed. Throughout our lives we freely talk about most chapters we have experienced. However, some are more difficult than others and we are reluctant to talk about them. But there is one chapter we never talk about. The last chapter: Death! It sounds so final. I have discovered this is the reason we are reluctant to talk about it.

We live in a culture that refuses to talk about death. Because of the inherent unpleasantness regarding death we avoid bringing up the topic. America is death phobic. This is due in part by the culture of silence surrounding death in America. As Nancy Duff has noted, "…people's inability to talk about death means that many of them experience dying in a way diametrically opposed to what they actually want."[1]

Dying is never easy. Dying well is even harder. Most people when facing the last season of life are not ready to leave. They have regrets that have not been healed. This makes a hard situation even harder. When you have unfinished business during this season of your life you will never feel ready to leave. Feeling ready to leave is an important component in order to experience peace during this transition time. The primary barriers to that peace are broken relationships that are shrouded in unforgiveness and no reconciliation, resulting in a lack of gratitude for life. This emotional and spiritual state leads to fear. Without a conscious and intentional act to change your circumstances these barriers will only grow more difficult. They will morph into spiritual and emotional monsters that cripple you, at which time the fear of dying will be all consuming.

Hiding in Plain Sight

The statement I hear most often is, "I'm afraid to die." This statement always has many meanings. Most often it means I am not ready to leave this life because I have unfinished business. The unfinished business almost always refers to a broken or estranged relationship. You will never experience peace facing death if you have bitterness, anger, and/or animosity toward a significant relationship that is important to you. If action is not taken to heal the relationship, sorrow turns into fear. This process does not always happen on a conscious level. If the significant relationship has been written-off for years you may not realize the emotional turmoil it is now causing. A sense of unfinished business can be on a subconscious level. You just know you are not ready to die.

I commend your courage for picking up and reading a book about death and dying. I know it is not easy. It is never easy to face death and everything that comes with it. What I can guarantee is this, if you will read and act upon the information in the coming chapters on forgiveness, reconciliation, and gratitude, you will experience a far more peaceful death. Everyone has heard of these concepts. Most people believe they understand these concepts. But few people act upon them. The emotional and spiritual monsters can only be destroyed with forgiveness and reconciliation. Because we all think we understand these concepts, we seldom apply them. It is as if they are hidden in plain sight. We know they are important, but we seldom use them to slay the monsters. The truth is most people do not fully understand them and consequently do not apply their power in circumstances where forgiveness is necessary.

Elisabeth Kubler-Ross points out in her book, *On Death and Dying*, "…dying nowadays is more gruesome in many ways, namely, more lonely, mechanical, and dehumanized; at times it is even difficult to determine technically when the time of death has occurred."[2]   In America, we have an epidemic of silence. No one wants to talk about death and dying. We live in a culture where death is viewed as taboo and any discussion of it is regarded as morbid.[3] This culture of silence creates real problems for the person dying and family members. With no one talking about the inevitable it leaves room only for fear, isolation, and emotional separation.

According to Stanford School of Medicine, 80% of Americans would prefer to die at home. However, 60% of Americans die in acute care hospitals, 20% in nursing homes and only 20% die at home. The designated 20% that die at home includes accidental deaths.[4] This is due in part by the culture of silence regarding death in America. If as a culture we did a better job of talking about death and dying, the percentage of people desiring to pass at home would increase. In Chapter Seven, I discuss the important differences in quality of life verses extended life. But let me say here, in the last months of a person's life, the quality of that life is paramount. This often becomes a battle ground between quality and extension of life.

Henri Nouwen was a Dutch Catholic priest, professor, writer, and theologian. He is well known for his work in pastoral ministry and spirituality. He points out in his book, *Life of the Beloved*, there is such a thing as a good death.[5] Nouwen describes two ways to view death. If we hold onto life too tightly then death becomes a failure. However, if we view life with open hands, we experience freedom, and this will bring hope to others. In other words, our death can become a gift. One of the best examples of this is Dr. Billy Graham, who died February 21, 2018 at the age of 99. He experienced a good death. He trusted that life is a preparation for death and should be the final act of giving. How a person dies is important. Looking at the available research, many people die with anger, bitterness, and contempt in their hearts. They die without forgiveness and the feeling of reconciliation with God, family, and other significant relationships.

Breaking the silence of death involves having conversations, and the overarching conversation needed is one of forgiveness. Spirituality plays an important role in forgiveness. Moreover, spirituality holds a special fascination for the dying and can ease the transition. Understanding the importance of spirituality in the dying process is often overlooked. In American culture there are numerous forms of spirituality: religious and non-religious. Each person must find spirituality in his or her own way. Regardless of how a person defines spirituality, it becomes the conduit for forgiveness of oneself, forgiveness of others, and potential reconciliation. I will discuss the importance of spirituality in Chapter Six.

In her book, *Sacred Dying*, Megory Anderson expresses the importance of forgiveness. She writes, "It is often just as hard to forgive someone for a past hurt as it is to admit wrongdoing and ask for forgiveness. When a person is dying, wrongdoing can weigh heavily on the conscience. When someone wants to put things right, asking for and receiving forgiveness is extremely important."[6] Forgiveness and reconciliation are the necessary elements to face death with inner peace and serenity. Why? Because forgiveness and reconciliation lead to a sense of gratefulness. When your heart is full of gratitude, it allows you to open your hands as a welcoming gesture. In other words, you are free to leave this life and to leave it well, having a sense of readiness.

To quote Nouwen again this time from his book, *Befriending Death*: "When we think about death, we often think about what will happen to us after we have died. But it is more important to think about what will happen to those we leave behind. The way we die has a deep and lasting effect on those who stay alive. It will be easier for our family and friends to remember us with joy and peace if we have said a grateful goodbye than if we die with bitter and disillusioned hearts."[7]

The best way to say to our families and friends that we love them is to have a heart full of gratitude. Giving this gift to the people we care about helps to set them free to go forward with their lives without bitterness or a crippling sense of loss. I will illustrate this with a personal story of my mother's passing. However, let me reiterate this important sequence: forgiveness and reconciliation are crucial for experiencing peace at the end of life. Unless a terminally ill person can find forgiveness and reconciliation in their heart, gratitude for their life will be elusive. Forgiveness and reconciliation open your heart to allow a sense of gratitude to be birthed. These components are not circular in nature. One does not lead to another. Think of the sequence like this; having experienced forgiveness and reconciliation becomes the superhighway for a sense of gratitude. Every broken and estranged significant social relationship in your life chips away at having a sense of gratitude. Gratitude for life allows for gratitude in death. Unfortunately, gratitude is difficult to experience without experiencing forgiveness and reconciliation. I have discovered in my work with the dying, experiencing forgiveness and reconciliation allows gratitude to come easier. Therefore, I encourage people to start there. This book will help you begin this important journey of forgiveness and reconciliation.

The components of forgiveness, reconciliation and gratitude are not necessarily more important than the other. Each component is equal in importance. They do, however, play very distinctive roles. These distinctive roles will be discussed in more detail in the coming chapters. It is essential to understand the importance of each component and how the sequencing acts as the glue that binds them together.

There are two important barriers in achieving the sequence mentioned above. First, is the unwillingness on the part of the person dying to seek forgiveness and reconciliation. It takes courage to reach out to people we have hurt or have hurt us. However, it is within this vulnerable position that the magic takes place and miracles happen. In Chapter Ten, the importance of vulnerability will be discussed. Second, to disregard the spiritual aspects of the human life. As I mentioned earlier, I am using the term spirituality in a broad sense. Every human being is spiritual. Whether you recognize this aspect of your humanness or not, it is indeed true. I will speak to this important issue in Chapter Eleven.

According to David Kessler, author of *The Needs of the Dying*, spirituality allows reaching into the purest part of ourselves: the part that is connected to love, the part that is connected to God, the part that is beyond the body and health or disease.[8] Spirituality is not concerned with the body; it is focused on the mind and spirit, although it is important to understand that spirituality affects the physical body. Overcoming fear of dying involves the mind and the spirit. When the mind finds rest, the spirit finds peace. Spirituality can accomplish both.

> Is death such an absolute end of all our thoughts and actions that we simply cannot face it? Or is it possible to befriend our dying gradually and live open to it, trusting that we have nothing to fear? Is it possible to prepare for our death with the same attentiveness that our parents had in preparing for our birth? Can we wait for our death as for a friend who wants to welcome us home?
>
> Henri Nouwen, *Our Greatest Gift*

The American approach to dying in the twenty-first century is one of silence. For most, the topic of death is a difficult issue to talk about. We live in an age of high-technology medicine. The advances in medicine over the last twenty-five years have been extraordinary. People have come to expect medications to cure their illnesses. Medical miracles have become the norm. New advancements in the science of medicine pushes the boundary between life and death. Modernized medicine and medications have turned death into a murky territory for many terminally ill patients.

In a culture of silence regarding the second most important event in life (dying), everyone is left confused and uncertain. The age-old question of what is a good death never gets answered. The terminally ill patient lives out their last months and weeks in fear and apprehension. Family members experience regret, anger, and unresolved issues with the passing of their loved one. In his book, *Befriending Death*, Henri Nouwen writes, "We are a fearful people. We are afraid of conflict, war, an uncertain future, illness, and, most of all, death. This fear takes away our freedom and gives our society the power to manipulate us with threats and promises."[9] Nouwen's words were never truer. During the COVID-19 pandemic millions of Americans are living in fear. A fear of an unseen enemy. The death rate continues to rise. The economic outlook is bleak. People are asking where do we go from here? I am not sure where America is heading. But I do know that a good place to start is with forgiveness, reconciliation, and a thankfulness for your life. These concepts seldom happen without one important ingredient, "conversation."

If the culture of silence regarding death in America is to change, health care professionals, clergy, social workers, family members and the patient must begin having the difficult conversations about dying. Fortunately, "Whole-person care" or "person-centered care" is a modern concept in health care and can help to reduce this culture of silence. Without focused and intentional conversations about end of life, experiencing a good death is highly unlikely. For a terminally ill patient to experience a good death or a peaceful death their concerns must be addressed.

There have been numerous studies where terminally ill patients have indicated what they think it means to die well. These studies reveal the top concerns people have. The top twelve concerns identified are:

- pain management (rated number one in most studies)
- clear decision-making
- avoidance of inappropriate prolongation of dying
- preparation for death
- relieving burdens
- strengthening relationships with loved ones
- a sense of completion
- contributing to others
- an affirmation as a whole person
- funeral arrangements made
- being mentally aware
- coming to peace with God[10]

If you read this list carefully, you will notice that nine out of twelve refer in some way to relationships. When these concerns are not addressed, the patients become increasingly fearful and worried about dying. They intuitively sense that their lives are incomplete. It is the feeling of unfinished business concerning one's life. These twelve concerns all involve having a conversation with the appropriate individuals. In my work with the dying, I often speak to patients receiving hospice care. Eight times out of ten they have little or no understanding of end-of-life issues. In addition to the importance of forgiveness, reconciliation, and gratitude, end-of-life planning is essential. Few patients have prepared for the legal side of dying. Death planning will be discussed in Chapters Thirteen and Fourteen.

Planning to Die

Elisabeth Kubler-Ross gave us the five stages on how most patients face dying. When they receive a terminal diagnosis there is denial and isolation. The second stage is anger, the third is bargaining, the fourth stage is depression, then finally acceptance. I believe it is possible to minimize the impact of each stage on the patient with conversation and education.[11] Kubler-Ross eloquently points out how we must begin.

> "If all of us would make an all-out effort to contemplate our own death, to deal with our anxieties surrounding the concept of our death, and to help others familiarize themselves with these thoughts, perhaps there could be less destructiveness around us."[12]

The destructiveness of dying without hope is the worst form of death. It is agony. With education and conversation, spiritual and emotional suffering can be minimized if not completely curtailed.

A Gallup poll that was conducted several years ago[13] determined the following major spiritual concerns in America:

Concern	% positive responses
Not being forgiven by God	56%
Not being reconciled with others	56%
Dying while being cut off or removed from God (higher power)	51%
Not being forgiven by someone for a past offense	49%
Not having a blessing from a family member or clergy	39%
The nature of the experience of death	39%

If we could start talking about end-of-life issues, each concern shown above can be substantially reduced, if not eliminated. For a person to die well, forgiveness, reconciliation, and a sense of gratitude must be present. These components are critical to the dying process. In addition, a good death involves planning. The use of advance directives is necessary and fosters the need for conversations. It is a win-win situation.

To Die Well

Dying well is a two-phase process. First, we have all heard the phrase, *"It is time to get my affairs in order."* This phrase, although an important notion, is seldom followed. People either are afraid to face death straight on and prepare for it, or they do not know how to prepare. Since no one is talking about the inevitable, the terminally ill patient is in a murky darkness.[14] Part of the murky darkness is caused by not having affairs in order. The advanced directives are important in easing the mind regarding final affairs. Specific legal documents will be discussed in Chapters Thirteen and Fourteen. When this step is overlooked, either by the patient, the family members or clinical staff, the terminally ill patient remains fearful and confused. In a 2013 survey 90 percent of people say that talking with their loved ones about end-of-life care is important. Unfortunately, only 27 percent had done so.[15] Unfortunately these numbers have not changed.

The second part to dying well is spiritual. Spirituality helps to open your heart to forgiveness and reconciliation. These two concepts are both horizontal and vertical. The importance of this phase cannot be overstated. For a terminally ill patient to die with dignity and peace they must know that their significant social relationships are in order. In addition, they need to know God forgives them. In *The Tibetan Book of Living and Dying*, Sogyal Rinpoche writes:

> "All religions stress the power of forgiveness, and this power is never more necessary, nor more deeply felt, than when someone is dying. Through forgiving and being forgiven, we purify ourselves of the darkness of what we have done, and prepare ourselves most completely for the journey through death."[16]

I have counseled many terminally ill patients and one thing they all have in common when nearing the end of life, when asked "what's on your mind" the answer always involves the people they love. The facing of death reveals our relationships to be our most precious possessions. Many terminally ill patients however still die feeling a lack of reconciliation and forgiveness. This is largely due to refusing to communicate about the dying process. The significance of spirituality on the end of life will be discussed further in Chapter Eleven.

According to Karen Swartz, M.D., director of the Mood Disorders Adult Consultation Clinic at the Johns Hopkins Hospital, chronic anger puts you into a fight-or-flight mode, which results in numerous changes in heart rate, blood pressure and immune response. Those changes then increase the risk of depression, heart disease and diabetes, among other conditions. Forgiveness, however, calms stress levels, leading to improved health.[17] Unresolved personal issues with significant social relationships often grow into deep-seated anger, furthering non-communication and perpetuating anxiousness in the dying process. Studies have found that some people are just naturally more forgiving. Consequently, they tend to be more satisfied with their lives and to have less depression, anxiety, stress, anger, and hostility. People who hang on to grudges however, are more likely to experience severe depression as well as other health conditions. According to the Fetzer Institute, 62 percent of American adults say they need more forgiveness in their personal lives. Imagine how this is multiplied when nearing death? End of life conversations must involve forgiveness and reconciliation between family members and close friends.

In addition to horizontal forgiveness there must be vertical forgiveness. For most terminally ill patients there comes a time when their concept of a higher power, or God, becomes important. There is a feeling it is time to make things right with God. Consequently, God's forgiveness becomes important. Unfortunately, many have a difficult time asking God to forgive them. Feelings of not being deserving of forgiveness or fearful of asking continues to perpetuate death anxiety.

The theoretical work of Erikson (1959)[18] and Butler and Lewis (1982)[19] shows why death anxiety may be an especially relevant outcome measure in research on forgiveness in late life. The final stage in Erikson's well-known theory of "life span development" deals with resolving the crisis of integrity versus despair. This is a time of deep introspection, where a person looks back over the life he or she has lived and attempts to accept the way things have turned out. If this stage is not resolved successfully a person can slip into despair, which often involves a "fear of death" and "high anxiety."

The silence about death and dying in the American culture comes with a high price. The terminally ill patient feels disconnected and without hope. The family members of the person dying, experience exacerbated feelings of guilt and grief. In the best circumstances, death is difficult. It is made far worse by silence. People die everywhere. Hospitals, skilled nursing facilities, prison and homes need to be places where death and dying conversations take place. Unless we have conversations about this topic, the central issues of forgiveness, reconciliation, and gratitude may never be discovered or acted upon. The focus of this book is to simply help you start talking about death and dying. Once the conversation begins, then the components of a good death can be addressed.

Rae's Story

Rae was a seventy-three-year-old female. She was also my mother. Ten years earlier she had been diagnosed with breast cancer. Consequently, both breasts had been removed and she lived cancer free. But the day she had dreaded for a decade finally came. The cancer was back and aggressive. Her doctors gave her six weeks to live. The news was devastating.

I had never talked with my mother about her death and she never brought it up. Like most people, the subject of death and dying was not a household conversational topic. I was not prepared to talk with my mother about it. Prepared or not, death was now the elephant in the room. And it was a big elephant. This was the first time I had ever intentionally felt a need to talk about death. This was a new experience.

By God's grace, we started to talk. She was afraid and full of regret. Absolutely no peace. My mother had grown up in Roseburg, Oregon and raised on a ranch. She was one of eight children. Her father was a taskmaster and forced hard labor on all his kids, with no exceptions. One older brother had run away and froze to death riding in a boxcar. Life was hard. The burdens of my mother's childhood never left her.

I was an only child and loved my mother dearly. I wanted to help her in this last chapter. Fortunately, I had never found it difficult to talk with her about my issues. This was not about me though; it was about her. I was about to lose her forever. I felt helpless but did manage to ask her how I could help. See looked into my eyes and I could see the fear. It was almost tangible. My heart was breaking. I asked her again, "Mom, how can I help?" She looked at me with tears and said, "Terry, I have three requests. First, I want to die here, in my home. I don't want to die in a hospital. Second, I don't want to be in pain and third, I want you with me." I was speechless.

Somehow, I got a few words out and told her I would make sure her requests were followed. The next day I called a local hospice organization and made arrangements for their services. This was my first experience with hospice. They were a godsend. Without their hospice nurse caring for my mother over those next few weeks, I would have been lost.

Even knowing that her three requests would be realized; she was still extremely fearful of dying. Over the next three weeks the cancer took over more and more of her body. Her body was preparing for the inevitable. Her mind, however, was in turmoil. Rae had not lived a life that was in any way preparing for a good death. Death was to be avoided. I had been a Christian most of my adult life and we would talk from time to time about God. Unfortunately, she never seemed to have interest in spiritual matters.

Two weeks before she died, I was talking with her about Christ and his redemptive love for her. We talked about forgiveness. Forgiveness toward her father for being so harsh and unloving. Forgiveness toward her mother for not protecting her. Forgiveness towards God for abandoning her. We also talked about reconciliation. I told her that God had never abandoned her, that he had been near her this whole time. Then I invited her to accept Christ into her heart and accept his forgiveness. To my delight, we prayed together for her to allow Jesus into her heart. I prayed, then she prayed. Her face was down, and she was sobbing. I put my arms around her and held her.

After several long minutes, she raised her head and I saw it. I have tears writing this. What I saw, I would not have believed if I had not experienced it. When she looked up, I saw a different woman. Where was my fearful mother? The woman sitting before me had changed. Changed in an instant. There was no more fear. The sobbing I watched and heard was not because of a life full of regrets. They were sobs of joy and gratitude. She had encountered Christ right before my eyes and was immediately filled with peace and thankfulness. It was remarkable. It was a spiritual healing. She had been set free.

My mother died two weeks later in my arms, peacefully.

I could have never imagined that twenty-one years after her death I would be writing a book on the importance of forgiveness, reconciliation, and gratitude during the dying process. I have discovered that this life is a preparation for the life to come.

The comedian and filmmaker Woody Allen once quipped: "I'm not afraid of death; I just don't want to be there when it happens." This, however, is not an option. You will, indeed, be there. We will all be there. I want to be there and be there fully. It has been said, "To die well, one must live well." I have learned the truth of this statement. I have discovered that God's "fingerprints" are present on our lives from beginning to end. Even when we do not realize it, He is present. I hope you can learn it too. As you read this book, remember that "Death is the Final Act of Love."

Chapter Six

HAVING THE CONVERSATION

"Let us make a special effort to stop communicating with each other, so we can have some conversation."

~ Mark Twain

I briefly talked about the "conversation" in the introduction. However, the topic is so important, I decided to dedicate a chapter to the topic. As I mentioned earlier, in American culture we do not talk about death. The subject is taboo. Can you remember the last time you had a serious talk about death with someone who is important in your life? Probably not. And I understand why that is. It is a difficult subject to talk about. That makes it even more important to talk about. Death and dying is difficult; it is also inevitable. Since no one gets out of this life alive, it is imperative we begin to have the "conversation". Ram Dass gives us a perfect example. He shares a story about his mother, and it makes an important point. Dass writes,

> "When I was in my 30s, my mother was diagnosed with a terminal blood disorder. I went to visit her in the hospital, and all the people around her were saying things like, 'You look great!' 'You'll be home in no time!' But she looked terrible, and it was likely she'd never come home again. No one, not my father, her sister or the rabbi would tell her the truth. In that moment I saw just how isolated she was. She

was dying and no one would talk to her about death. We spoke about it, Soul to Soul, and she began to relax."[20]

When we refuse to talk about death, we are exacerbating the fear and anxiety of the terminally ill. I am not trying to over-simplify the emotional suffering that comes with facing death. It is not easy. American culture sees death as the enemy and therefore must be hidden or shunned. Consequently, the inherent emotional difficulty that comes with end-of-life is exacerbated.

Without adequate privacy and inviting décor, the likeliness of everyone engaging in conversations about death and dying are diminished, if not completely ignored. Without the necessary engagement between family members and the terminally ill person the culture of silence is perpetuated, and people die in fear and anxiety.

Once again, the words of Kubler-Ross echo the truth of the dying process. People are dying... "more lonely, mechanical, and dehumanized."[21] This book can provide support for the entire family and deal with the social, emotional, and spiritual issues that surround end of life. I will also help individuals have the necessary conversations. If the patient and family members are disinclined to talk about death everyone loses. Having appropriate and specific conversations about end-of-life with all parties concerned is imperative.

Breaking the culture of silence around death and dying is the gateway to helping terminally ill patients understand their spirituality. This book will develop a methodology for breaking the silence and using spirituality to bring inner peace through a heart of forgiveness, reconciliation, and gratitude. Henri Nouwen writes in, *Our Greatest Gift:*

"Is death such an absolute end of all our thoughts and actions that we simply cannot face it? Or is it possible to

befriend our dying gradually and live open to it, trusting
that we have nothing to fear? Is it possible to prepare for
our death with the same attentiveness that our parents had
in preparing for our birth? Can we wait for our death as for
a friend who wants to welcome us home?"

When I was in high school, I enjoyed reading the great philosophers like Plato and Aristotle. They wrestled with questions that intrigued. Questions about virtue and honor, importance of community, about what a good life should consist of, and what a good death should look like.   I remember reading Socrates, who stated, "Philosophy is ultimately a preparation for death." What constitutes a good life? What constitutes a good death? One should define the other.

The American approach to dying in the twenty-first century is one of silence. For most, the topic of death is a difficult issue to talk about. We live in an age of high-technology medicine. The advances in medicine over the last twenty-five years have been extraordinary. People have come to expect medications to cure their illnesses. Medical miracles have become the norm. New advancements in the science of medicine push the boundary between life and death. Modernized medicine and medications have turned death into a murky territory for many terminally ill patients.

In a culture of silence regarding the second most important event in life (dying), everyone is left confused and uncertain. The age-old question of what is a good death never gets answered. The terminally ill patient lives out their last weeks and days in fear and apprehension. Family members experience regret, anger, and unresolved issues with the passing of their loved one. In his book, *Befriending Death*, Nouwen writes, "We are a fearful people. We are afraid of conflict, war, an uncertain future, illness, and, most of all, death. This fear takes away our freedom and gives our society the power to manipulate us with threats and promises."[22]

My goal is about helping terminally ill patients and their families have conversations about end-of-life care. More specifically, my focus is on helping terminally ill patients die without fear and anxiety while helping family members understand and cope with their loss. This lack of communication about dying is not only among non-medical care givers. Physicians and nurses find it difficult to talk about death. Angelo E. Volandes, a physician and researcher at Harvard Medical School and Massachusetts General Hospital explains:

> "In 2008, a group of Dartmouth researchers surveyed all 128 U.S. medical schools regarding offerings in "Palliative and Hospice Care." Of the forty-eight medical schools that responded to the survey, only fourteen had a required course and only nine had a mandatory rotation on the subject. Seven schools offered an elective course and fourteen had an optional rotation for students that were interested in the topic. The researchers concluded that only a small fraction of U.S. medical schools required training in communicating with patients with advanced, incurable conditions."[23]

If the culture of silence regarding death in America is to change, health care professionals, clergy, social workers, family members and the patient must begin having the difficult conversations about dying. Fortunately, "whole-person care" or "person-centered care" is a modern concept in health care and can help to reduce this culture of silence. Without focused and intentional conversations about end of life, experiencing a good death is highly unlikely. For a terminally ill patient to experience a good death or a peaceful death, their concerns must be addressed. Geoffrey Gorer, a British sociologist has written about death and writes, "the subject of death has become as unmentionable as sex was during Victorian times." Talking about death with the people who are closest to us is crucial if we are to change the way we die.

It is imperative that we know how our loved ones feel about death. We need to share our fears, our hopes, our beliefs about dying. Otherwise, people continue to live in the shadowlands of death. Meaning, they live confused, fearful, and frustrated as they attempt to navigate this forbidden realm. This is particularly true at the end of life. Moreover, it forces loved ones to guess and speculate about what the terminally ill person needs and wants. Maybe you think, even without conversations about death, you know exactly what your loved one wants regarding their death. Relying on your assumptions is dangerous. Research shows that most people appointed as health care agents/proxies have no clear idea what the person wants. Shooting in the dark with something as important as dying is extremely careless, especially if it is last minute. Waiting until the end to have discussions about death makes it even more difficult.

If you talk about death and dying when all parties are reasonably healthy, the "D" subject is generally easier to talk about. Even if the conversations do not go well, at least the subject matter has been put on the table. This will make it easier when the "D" conversation is crucial. If you have had some talks about death it will be less difficult to ask the tough questions, get information, and make hard decisions as death approaches. These conversations should involve loved ones and the care team professionals. Dr. Elisabeth Kubler-Ross calls death "the last and greatest taboo." I hope my book will help you to demystify the topic of death and dying and begin to have conversations with our loved ones.

How do you effectively begin talking about this topic with loved ones? How do you mention the word "death" to someone you love? Can you hear yourself saying, "(their name) what are your thoughts on dying?" I assure you I understand the courage it takes. I have had hundreds of conversations about death with people and it never is easy. Dying is hard work. But it is much harder without having talked about it. If you are concerned about how your death will be handled, choose your health care agent or a trusted friend and begin having conversations about your views and values about death. Getting someone to talk about their views regarding death, is more difficult. If you are the instigator of the conversation, be patient and sensitive. However, the sooner the better because it will take time to cover all the necessary ground. The longer this conversation is put-off, the harder it becomes. Having these conversations before death is imminent makes it easier. If the "D" horizon is clearly in view, then take a breath and with a gentle tone begin the conversation.

You might start talking about advance directives and how important they are. You might begin the conversation talking about your views and what you want for your death. You could use a third party, like a friend, and have them talk about their experiences with death. How you start the conversation is not as important as starting it. If nothing works, ask a friend or relative to broach the topic with your loved one. You could ask the person's physician or attorney or pastor to start the conversation. Do your best to initiate the first conversation in a space where you will not be interrupted, distracted, or hurried. Before you initiate, think through what you want to say and be willing to listen carefully to the responses of the other person. Conversations about death may be awkward at first. Be patient. Do not allow yourself to feel defeated. Be prayerful.

The concept of death takes in a lot of territory. It is a conversation as much about life as it is death. It involves getting to know the other person on a deep level. Their fears and concerns about the most intimate of all human experiences – death. If you are like me, as you are having these conversations, you will feel very privileged. This will not be a "one time" conversation. Generally, your discussions will be ongoing. It will take numerous conversations with your loved one to fully understand their views and values and preferences. Then when you think you fully understand, they change. So, let me say again, be patient. Be patient with your loved one and yourself.

The Devil Is in the Details

Maybe you have heard this phrase. "The devil is in the details" an idiom that refers to the mysterious elements often found in the fine points. In other words, something might seem simple at first glance, but will take more time and effort to complete. This concept certainly applies to death and dying. It is in the details if you or your loved one are to experience a good death. A peaceful death. This is why having appropriate conversations are vital. It is within those conversations the details come into view. Throughout this book, you will be reading about the details regarding a good death. One way to determine what some of those details look like is to imagine the situation and then make a list. List all of your concerns. After you list your concerns, then write out how to address them. You can do this for yourself or someone else.

I encourage you to create a file. In the file, you will have all the information that your designated agent will need. Once you have all the necessary information in the file, keep it in a safe place. Make sure your healthcare agent/proxy knows while the file is kept. Keep the file updated. Here are a few ideas for your file:

✓ **Who should be contacted:**

When you die, who should be informed? Make a list of friends with phone numbers and instruct your agent to contact them. This is a more personal touch rather than having someone read about your passing in the obituaries. Other possibilities could be business partners or associates, attorneys, physicians, brokers, pension, and insurance agents.

Keep in mind, financial institutions and others may need a certificate of death.

✓ Personal property:

I highly encourage you to have a copy of your "Last Will & Testament" in this file. Your will is going to instruct how you want your personal property handled. You can give general instructions verbally to your family regarding items like jewelry, personal letters, books, your diary, dishes, etc.

Remember, in some states verbal Wills that meet the legal requirements are binding, although it is wiser to put everything in writing.

✓ Personal finances:

Does anyone know where you keep your important papers? Documents such as your original will, insurance policies, checkbook, tax returns, investments and bank information, credit and debit cards, titles, and deeds to real property.

Do you have a safe-deposit box? If so, who should have access to the key? Do you have important financial information on your computer? If so, your agent or a family member will need the passwords.

✓ Business interest:

Who will be responsible for settling your business dealings? Are there outstanding invoices to be paid? Is there anyone who owns your business money? Someone needs to take care of unfinished paperwork, business ledgers, receipts, contracts, rental agreements, etc.

What about your office supplies or research information or any unfinished manuscripts?

✓ **Children under 18**:

If there are young children and both parents die, who will care for the children? Naming a guardian in a will is a good first step. Make sure the person named is willing to care for the children and understands any special needs they may have.

How will the children be supported financially? Has a trust been established? These questions can lead to complicated legal issues. That is why it is important to address these questions early on. If you have small children, you might write them letters and/or make videos for them, in the event something happens to you.

✓ **Funeral and burial:**

What are your desires about your funeral and burial arrangements? As with weddings, there are many details to planning a funeral. I have listed a few of the questions you need to think about.

> - Are there specific songs or hymns you want?
> - Are there poems, or literary readings you would like?
> - Do you have particular clergy you would like involved? Do they know your desires?
> - Where do you want to be buried?
> - Do you want to be cremated? If so, where do you want your ashes placed?
> - How should your obituary read? What do you want included?
> - Who will publish your obituary?
> - How will your funeral and burial be paid for? Should it be paid in advance?
> - Do you want flowers?
> - Will there be a reception? If so, where, when, and who will organize it?

Something to keep in mind is that funerals are for the living. While your suggestions are important, especially if you feel strongly about something, you will not be attending. Your survivors will be. Think about what might be important to them. An important part of the grieving process is saying good-bye. The planning of a funeral is part of that process. So, you do not have to plan every detail. Leave room for your family and friends to find their own ways to express their love for you.

✓ Organ donation:

This can be a tricky subject for loved ones to deal with. It may be something they have never thought about. If they are going through a time of grieving, organ donation will be something they cannot imagine. That is why it is important for you to make your wishes known. You need to communicate how you feel about organ donation and your preferences.

Healthy lungs, kidneys, hearts, corneas, skin are desperately needed in our country. If you are interested, sign the organ donor portion of your driver's license, and make sure you let your family know your wishes. For more information go to www.organdonor.gov.

✓ The forgotten details:

What about your private matters? Do you have diaries or letters that you do not want others to see? Who will be responsible for your private matters? Who will take care of your special pet(s) or rare plants? I am sure you can think of more details that will need attention.

Are you beginning to see how important having the "conversation" really is? There is so much that needs to be talked about and worked through. My motivation for writing this book was to help people experience a good death – a peaceful death. A death that leaves behind a wonderful legacy. It all begins with talking! Just talking! But talking specifically about death and related issues is the key. So, let us begin having "the conversation."

First, let's talk about some misconceptions. Understanding what is not true will help you engage with the topic of death either for yourself or for a loved one. Often going through a death experience with a friend or loved one often changes the relationship. The change can either be good or bad. It may draw you closer with the person or it may push the relationship in a negative direction. It can be extremely difficult to talk with a dying loved one. You will probably find yourself thinking, "What do I say?" or "I may upset them talking about death." There are several common misconceptions that hinder us bringing up the topic of death.

> ✓ **Talking about death will lead to despair:**

It is a commonly held notion that talking about someone's illness or impending death will certainly upset them. The truth is most people facing a severe illness or impending death want to talk about it. However, they are often afraid to bring it up, fearing it will upset their friend or loved one.

Most people with a terminal illness want and need to talk about how they are feeling. They need to express their fears and concerns. I have found that when I listen closely and without judgment, it helps the person reduce their anxieties. This is called the Ministry of Presence. Just being present with someone and willing to listen is a true gift.

> ✓ **Talking about death and dying will only exacerbate an already difficult situation:**

Another misconception is the belief that talking about death will actually cause it to happen sooner. They may feel that discussing death will increase the stress on the dying person and could result in additional health problems such as a heart attack or stroke. Moreover, talking about death to a dying person may cause that person to accept their death and give up wanting to live. Consequently, they die sooner.

Nothing could be further from the truth. Early in the 20th century it was common to be told by a physician not to share a terminal diagnosis with an elderly patient because it would certainly hasten their death. Obviously, talking about death can be stressful, but it can also be therapeutic. It can bring a sense of acceptance and courage.

Compassion and gentleness should always be the tone of the conversation. Be sensitive to the dying person and refuse to allow your feelings to burden them any further. Be careful not to place your grief upon them.

✓ **Whatever I talk about will be harmful:**

Often, we feel that talking about daily events will be hurtful. Example: You may feel that having a conversation about your favorite book or movie with your loved one communicates that you do not care about what they are going through. You tell yourself they could not possibly care about those kinds of things anymore.

On the contrary, most terminally ill people are still interested in the same things they were interested in before they knew they were dying. If your loved one was a sports enthusiast prior to their illness, their enjoyment of sports is probably still present. Moreover, I can assure you that your loved one is still interested in you. Tell them about what is going on in your life. Talking about every day events helps your loved one realize they are still alive and part of your life.

✓ **Silence is stressful:**

There is an ancient proverb that states, "Speech is silver, and silence is golden." You have probably heard the last part of this proverb. Silence is golden. Meaning, there are times when keeping your mouth closed is a good thing. We all know people who have a difficult time not talking. Being with a dying loved one or friend is no time to fill the air with empty words. Sometimes it is better to be a listener rather than a talker. Silence does not have to be awkward. This goes back to the Ministry of Presence. Just being physically present can be calming.

Be willing to be in the moment. Be present. Give the dying person your full attention, even if you are not talking. Fully listening can help open-up communication. Here are a few tips on how to listen well:

> ➤ Be respectful – do not force your viewpoints onto the dying person. This is their experience but be willing to journey alongside of them.

> ➤ Be honest – resist the need to search for the right thing to say. Do not try to be clever. Be yourself. Remember, dying is a profound process and everyone has different needs. Simply holding a hand can be soothing for a dying person.

> ➤ Use positive body language – This may seem like common sense, but under the circumstances can be difficult. Remember to look your loved one or friend in the eye when talking or listening. Be alert and attentive. Pay attention to what they are saying. Listen carefully to their tone of voice and watch their facial expressions.

> ➤ Their body language – Watch their body language to help determine what they are saying is what they mean. If you

perceive a disconnect, invite them to share what is really on their minds.

➢ Remain calm – It is not unusual to feel uneasy with this level of emotional intimacy. Seeing a loved one or friend so vulnerable can be difficult. Often there are tears and volatile emotions. Stay calm and breathe.

➢ Listening while talking – if the conversation becomes difficult, remember these tips:

   o Indirect questions: If you feel it is appropriate, you can ask questions like, "Is there something bothering you that you would like to talk about?" or "Is there anything I can do to help you in this moment?" Asking these types of questions gives your loved one or friend the availability to respond or say no. When you provide a *choice*, you are empowering your loved one or friend. Even if they do not respond at the moment, they know the door is open and could come back to the question later. It also communicates you are a safe person to talk with.

   o Leading questions: Another approach is to ask questions in such a way that the answer is specific and direct. Examples: "If you become really sick, would you like for me to sit with you?" or "If your illness becomes worse, what kind of medication would you like?" "Have you thought about what kind of funeral you would like?" Once again, this provides the dying person the choice whether to respond or not.

> ➤ Tears in the quietness – Remember, it is okay to cry. It is okay to be quiet. These are emotional moments. Showing your grief can have a powerful and positive effect on the relationship. This goes both ways. It is the same for you and the dying person. You both need permission to grieve.

Overcoming the Fear of Talking About Death

As I have already stated, we do not talk about death and dying in American culture. It is not only loved ones and friends of the dying person who find it difficult to talk about death. The dying themselves often find it difficult to express what they are feeling and what they need. There are many reasons why this subject is hard to talk about. Notwithstanding the difficulty, without having the appropriate conversations about death, everyone loses. Everyone is deprived of the peace that comes with acceptance. As I previously stated, a peaceful death is possible, and it begins with "the conversation."

Why loved ones and friends find it hard to talk about death:

- Fear of saying the wrong thing and making the situation worse
- Fear of loss
- Fear of what other relatives might think or say
- The notion that health care professionals know best
- Fear of their own mortality
- Guilt/shame about what has happened in the past
- Denial – "I just can't face the thought of losing them."
- Refusing reality (cannot face the truth, pretending everything is all right)

Why the dying find it hard to talk about death:

- Fear of being a burden to family and friends
- Lack of privacy, particularly in hospital wards
- Inner conflict and unfinished business
- Secrets that have never been shared

- Denial – "I can't face the truth."
- Fear of unsettling loved ones
- Not a talker
- Trusting the right person (A dying person may choose who they want to communicate with. It may not be a loved one or friend)

These are just a few reasons why the dying and their loved ones find it difficult to talk about death. As important as having "the conversation" is, it is also important to not push too hard on anyone who refuses to talk about this issue. Everyone processes death in different ways. Be patient, but do not give up attempting to have the talk. Some people are fortunate in their ability to approach their dying process with peace; however, they are the exception. Generally, people facing death are frightened, confused, and unable to clearly express what they are feeling and need. Under the chaotic emotions, dying people want the same thing that we all want, to be understood and accepted.

Some reasons for the chaotic emotions of the dying:

- They may be afraid to die
- They may feel they are a burden to loved ones and/or friends
- They may be angry at the thought of being cheated of life
- They may feel lost and alone
- They may feel angry at God for letting them down
- They may be hanging onto the hope of a miracle cure
- They may feel they wasted their life and are grieving missed opportunities
- They may be desperate to die
- They may want to contact ex-partners or estranged family or friends
- They may want to confess to things that have happened in the past, or to ask for forgiveness
- They may become irrationally angry, blaming, and resenting healthcare workers and the world at large

- They may be missing relatives and friends who are unable to be with them

As you have been reading this chapter, you are probably beginning to sense the importance of talking about death and dying with friends and family. In addition, it is my hope you have realized the sooner you begin death and dying conversations, the more likely you will enjoy the benefits. I will talk more about the benefits in forthcoming chapters. Before we move on, I want to share with you one practical idea on how to begin conversations about death. As I have said, the sooner you begin this process the more beneficial it will be. Whether you are thinking about your own death, the death of a loved one or friend, the time to begin is now.

Michael Hebb, in his delightful book entitled, *Let's Talk About Death over Dinner*, gives practical ideas on how to start having conversations about death and dying. Hebb gives you prompts that lead to interesting discussions. The prompts help you broach every aspect of end-of-life care. And you do it over dinner. The success of Hebb's approach is because it is intentional and conducted in a safe environment with humor and sensitivity. For more information go to www.deathoverdinner.org.

I hope I have conveyed the importance of communication when it comes to death and dying. Equally important is the content of your communications. I know I have given you a lot to think about in this chapter regarding having conversations. Besides the art of communicating, it is imperative that the next three chapters on forgiveness, reconciliation, and gratitude are part of your life. I will say over and over, to die well you must live well. It is impossible to live well without these three attributes functioning in your life. So, let us begin this journey of forgiveness, reconciliation, and a heart full of gratitude.

Chapter Seven

THE ROAD TO FREEDOM: FORGIVENESS

"Let what distracts you cease. Let what divides you cease. Let there come an end to what diminishes and demeans, and let depart all that keeps you in its cage."

~ Jan Richardson

Arguably the concept of forgiveness in the human experience is what it means to be human. However, this concept as powerful as it is, remains elusive for many. When a person experiences a life-threatening illness it often forces a review of one's life. During this review process we revisit the relationships that are important to us and often there are some regrets regarding one or more of these relationships. A life-threatening illness forces us to assess what is important in our lives. Important relationships that are broken, estranged, or alienated become barriers to finding peace at the end of life. According to Ivan Urli, "Forgiveness is central to healthy human development and may be one of the most important processes in the restoration of interpersonal relationship after conflict."[24]

So, what exactly is forgiveness? We have all heard of the concept. But do we really understand it? Forgiveness is a pro-social emotional response to a hurtful or harmful experience. The ability to truly forgive another human being for a harm they have caused is the only way to stay emotionally and spiritually healthy. Here is the interesting piece. Human beings are created with this ability. Every person alive on planet earth can forgive. It is part of your DNA. Unfortunately, many people *choose* not to. They ignore the power that forgiveness brings. The power to be set free from the burden of bitterness, anger, resentment, and the anguish these feelings bring with them. I call them the monsters of the soul. The power of forgiveness will be explored in detail later in this chapter.

Social Relationships

Hospice physician Ira Byock would often ask his patients, "If you were to die today, God forbid, but if you were to die today, is there anything that would be left undone?" The answer has become a cliché, but no one ever looks back over life and says, "I wish I had spent more time working." Far more often we look back and see hurts we have received from others or have given to others. The fabric of our lives is held together by our social relationships. Family and friends who have played a significant role in how we process the world around us become the glue that holds us together. When that fabric is broken or destroyed, we begin to unravel emotionally. This can begin at an early age. So, we develop emotional mechanisms to relieve the disconnect. Mechanisms such as narcissism, addictions, and in some cases a complete break from the ability to empathize with another. We will look at these barriers of forgiveness later in this chapter.

Lewis B. Smedes writes, "When we forgive, we set a prisoner free and discover that the prisoner we set free is us."[25] Forgiveness is the way to move beyond life's hurt and failures. When there is no resolution to a broken relationship, a particularly significant personal relationship, facing end-of-life becomes far more difficult. A terminally ill patient will find inner freedom by releasing hatred, anger, and thoughts of revenge. Forgiveness gives birth to this freedom. Without a sense of freedom there is no peace.

I do not want to oversimplify the deep struggles within the individual heart as end-of-life approaches. Yet from personal observation and years of research in this area I am convinced that the continuous practice of forgiveness can be experienced throughout life. Grasping and controlling individuals tend to be so to the very end of life. Those who live life with a sense of gratitude and grace also tend to do so to the very end.[26]   I will explore the importance of a heart full of gratitude later in Chapter Nine.

In his book, *The Troubled Dream of Life*, Daniel Callahan writes,

> "How we die will be an expression of how we have wanted to live, and the meaning we find in our dying is likely to be at one with the meaning we have found in our living...[A] person who has learned how to let life go may have not only a richer and more flexible life, but also one that better prepares him for his decline."[27]

Every significant social relationship you have is an interpersonal resource.   These relational resources are so important to your emotional and mental functioning, their relevance cannot be overstated. Put simply, you and I need social contact. Isolation and social retreating are dangerous to your mental and physical health. Consequently, when these significant social relationships are broken or impaired, your relational resources are depleted. This depletion causes conscious and subconscious harm.   Depending on the importance of the relationship, it will have a direct effect on how much emotional harm is done.

The Other Side of Forgiveness

The way we look at life and death ultimately effects how we live. After all, even though we may be preparing to die, we continue to live. This is not only true in understanding the power in accepting forgiveness, but it also brings into perspective the other side of forgiveness.

The other side of forgiveness is to ask to be forgiven for a wrong we have done to another. Everyone is capable of inflicting harm. Our actions and our words can all be used as weapons. Human beings have a tremendous ability to weaponize thoughts, words, and behaviors. This weaponization can be as destructive and crippling as any lethal weapon. In fact, in some cases it does far more damage. It is likely, during a lifetime, everyone has hurt someone else. The way to release this burden is to ask for forgiveness. Once again, the words of Lewis B. Smedes are most appropriate:

> The most creative power given to the human spirit is the power to heal the wounds of a past it cannot change. We do our forgiving alone inside our hearts and minds; what happens to the people we forgive depends on them. The first person to benefit from forgiving is the one who does it...Forgiving happens in three stages: We rediscover the humanity of the person who wronged us, we surrender our rights to get even, and we wish that person well...Forgiving does not require us to reunite with the person who broke our trust...Waiting for someone to repent before we forgive is to surrender our future to the person who wronged us...Forgiving is not a way to avoid pain but to heal pain...We do not excuse the person we forgive.

When we forgive, we set a prisoner free and discover that the prisoner we set free is us.[28]

Forgiveness, whether we are forgiving someone else or desiring another to forgive us, is a powerful force. It can bring healing and freedom to the human spirit. It is this freedom that allows the door to be opened for a person to experience peace at the end of life.

Forgiving Yourself

It has been said the greatest act of forgiveness is forgiving ourselves. Self-forgiveness may well be the greatest act of forgiveness because it is the hardest to accomplish. Making peace with yourself and moving forward can be a difficult task. Forgiving yourself requires you making a choice. You must choose to forgive yourself. The same compassion and understanding you would extend to another person you must extend to yourself. We all make mistakes. We are all imperfect. Making blunders is part of life. The real issue is how we deal with them. Do I allow a failure to define me? Mistakes and failures in life can cripple you. You become stuck in the past, reliving the mistakes over and over.

So how do we forgive ourselves? It begins with a choice. You must determine that you genuinely want to forgive yourself. Once that choice is made, then the work of self-forgiveness begins. You must remember to have patience with yourself. Never confuse your mistakes with your value as a human being. You are an extremely valuable, creative, worthwhile person simply because you exist. You have heard the phrase, "Anything of value takes work." Finding self-forgiveness has high value for you and will take work. But it will be worth it.

Once you make a choice to forgive yourself, you must begin taking an inventory of your inner life. Evaluate your emotions. You need to acknowledge them. Give yourself permission to evaluate and process what you are feeling. If you made a mistake and just cannot seem to let it go, acknowledge the mistake verbally. Say it out loud. This works to help free you from the burdens of the mistake. As you give a voice to the thoughts in your head and the emotions in your heart, it helps to free you. It is within this freedom that you can learn from your mistakes and move forward.

We all have an inner critic. Most of us do not enjoy being criticized. But in the case of our inner critic, you should pay attention. Journaling can be an important tool here. Write out the conversation between you and your inner critic. This process can help to identify thought patterns that are sabotaging your ability to forgive yourself. Journaling can help quiet the negative messages of your inner critic as well. Sometimes, however, it can be difficult to recognize the thoughts that are hindering our self-forgiveness. Here is an exercise that can help with identifying those thoughts.

On one side of your journal, write down what your inner critic is saying. Thoughts that are critical and irrational. On the other side of your journal, write out a self-compassionate and rational response for each entry that was critical. You might be surprised by what you learn. It is possible that some of the criticism is valid. If it is, then take it to heart and learn from it. With a little humility, constructive criticism can teach us valuable lessons. If the voice of your inner critic is not constructive or has merit, give yourself permission to disregard it.

Journaling your thoughts and your inner critic can help you to stop playing old tapes. It is human nature to spend time and energy replaying our mistakes and failures in our heads. Obviously, some processing is important. However, going over the mistake again and again will derail the forgiveness process. When you catch yourself playing the "I am a horrible person" tape, stop yourself and redirect your thinking. Take a walk, listen to music, call a friend. Do whatever it takes to see a new perspective. My personal favorite is to remind myself how God sees me. We are told in the Gospel of John that we are his children.[29] When I remind myself that God loves me no matter what, that there is nothing I can do to force him to forsake me, I am encouraged.

Practical Steps Towards Self-Forgiveness

Besides journaling, there are practical steps you can take to help you forgive yourself. The act of forgiveness, whether you are forgiving yourself or someone who has harmed you, does not mean you condone the hurtful events. It simply means that you have accepted the behavior, whether yours or someone else's, and you want to move forward. Self-forgiveness is about desiring to move beyond the past and focusing on the present. This becomes important at the end of life. Some people find it much easier to forgive others rather than themselves. Forgiving yourself paves the road to freedom.

The first step is to take responsibility. If you keep making excuses for your actions, self-forgiveness will be elusive. Continuing to justify the hurt you have caused will only perpetuate your inner self-loathing. You must face your actions honestly. Take responsibility, as difficult as it is, and decide to move forward. This acceptance will help you to avoid negative emotions, such as shame and guilt.

The second step is to allow yourself to experience remorse. Are you genuinely sorry for your actions? If you can answer this question in the affirmative, then your guilt can be turned into a positive feeling. Even though guilt feels terrible, it can serve to create positive behavioral change. The feeling of guilt means you made a mistake. Everyone makes mistakes. Good people make mistakes. The feeling of shame, however, makes you feel like a bad person.   Even though both feelings are often present, guilt can be used for positive changes and shame makes you feel worthless. Guilt can lead to behavior change. Shame can lead to addictions and depression. Therefore, self-forgiveness is important.

The third step is to repair the brokenness. The desire to make amends is important in the forgiveness process. However, there are times when this is impossible. As you read my story of regret, you will see the importance of not waiting to make things right. As you read this third step, you may be thinking this only benefits the person you harmed. But nothing could be further from the truth. Repairing emotional brokenness with another person is a two-way street. In fact, it may be more freeing for you than for the person you hurt. When you reach out and ask for forgiveness from someone you harmed, they may or may not accept your apology. That is their choice. But an honest attempt to fix your mistake will pay huge emotional dividends for you.

The fourth step is to focus on restoration. Everyone makes mistakes. It is part of being human. However, being trapped by self-hatred and pity will only damage your self-esteem and self-worth. Both are damaging to your emotional and mental state. Forgiving yourself will involve understanding why you acted the way you did. When you identify the "whys" of your actions, you can learn from them and grow as a person. Then you can take the necessary steps to avoid such behavior in the future.

If all or part of these steps are unable to be accomplished, you may become stuck in your feelings of guilt and shame. Without some intervention, it is possible to live this way for the rest of your life. Many people do and suffer the consequences. I lived this way for ten years. Let me tell you about one of my major regrets.

A Personal Story of Regret

My parents divorced when I was eight years old. However, they stayed good friends throughout the years. In 1983 they had decided to take a trip together. They were in Portland, Oregon when my father suffered a major stroke. Since my father was a Korean war veteran, he went to the VA hospital in Portland. After exhausting his VA benefits regarding his hospital stay, he had to be moved. I was an only child, so the responsibility fell to me. I flew up to Portland from southern California and brought my father back to an assisted living facility in Visalia, California. The stroke had paralyzed the right side of his body making it impossible to walk without assistance or a wheelchair. He also had great difficulty speaking. He would require personal assistance the rest of his life. When we arrived at the facility, I helped him out of the car into a wheelchair. I rolled him into the foyer and was met by an employee who immediately pushed him down the hall, presumably to his room. As he was being taken away, I said goodbye, but did not follow. There was no kiss, no handshake, no hand on the shoulder with endearing words. Only a spoken goodbye as he left my sight.

The reason for my lack of engagement was because I was completely self-absorbed. In honesty, I did not have time to spend with him. I had just graduated from Oregon State University and was moving to Hawaii the next day. My mind was completely focused on the move and myself. My selfishness had overshadowed any affection I felt for my father. I would not allow anyone or anything to disrupt my plans for this adventure. The depth of my selfishness during this time would become my deepest regret. As planned, I left the next day from Los Angeles and flew to Honolulu to begin my new life. My father barely crossed my mind. I was self-absorbed with doing exactly what I wanted to do.

I had been living in Hawaii for six months when early one morning the phone rang. When I picked up the receiver and said hello, I heard a female voice who calmly informed me that my father had died a few hours earlier. I was stunned. Speechless. The enormous weight of the guilt seemed to hit me like a bus. I could not move. I hung up the phone and wept. Then the shame poured over me like a cascading waterfall. My self-absorption had finally become clear. How could I have abandoned my father when he needed me most? I lived with that question for ten years.

For ten years I lived with the guilt and shame of the prodigal son. There were moments when this failure of character drove me to my knees. My soul would cry out for redemption. However, redemption was elusive. I was unable to forgive myself for the complete carelessness of my behavior towards my father. As the years went by, my self-loathing only increased. I was broken deep within my soul. And I was the only one that new how much it hurt. The depth of my despair was securely locked away in my heart. I deserved the pain. Even though it crippled me emotionally in many ways, I deserved it. I should suffer. Forgiving myself was impossible, until one day.

The year was 1994 and I had just graduated from law school. I was living in Bakersfield, California studying for the bar exam. It was a Sunday and I decided to take a drive. I drove east toward the foothills along the Kern River. I had been driving about an hour when all of sudden I began to cry. As the tears rolled down my face, I physically felt a hand on my right shoulder. I glanced over to my right and saw nothing. Then I felt the words, "I forgive you." In that instant I knew God had forgiven me for my behavior towards my father. Moreover, in that instant I was able to forgive myself. Then I realized my tears were tears of joy and not despair. This all happened in flash of time. But the experience was transformative. It changed my life. I have never had another encounter like that since that day.

The Need for God's Forgiveness

Forgiveness is both vertical and horizonal. Meaning, forgiveness forms a cross in the direction it flows. There is horizonal forgiveness that is necessary between individuals. There is vertical forgiveness that is necessary between individuals and God. In both cases, forgiveness flows back and forth respectively. Not only do you need to forgive yourself, extend and receive the forgiveness of others, but you need to receive God's forgiveness as well. In many cases you need to forgive Him for perceived harms He has allowed in your life.

Whatever the cases may be, embracing God's forgiveness is important. It opens the doorway for so many good and positive things. God's forgiveness opens your heart for possibilities you may never have imagined. I like to say, "you were made for God's forgiveness." If you have ever watched a football game on television, you have probably seen someone with a banner that states, "John 3:16." This is arguably the most famous passage in the New Testament. Here is what it says, For God so loved the world that He gave His one and only Son, that whoever believes in Him shall not perish but have eternal life. God stands ready to forgive you for past, present, and future sins. How amazing is that? If you read part one, then you will recall how I discovered the truth of John 3:16.

God's unconditional love articulated in the above verse is a difficult concept for people to accept. We have all learned that there is always a payment for something we receive. Nothing in this world is free. That is what we are taught from an early age. It is probably true except for God's grace and unconditional love. Fortunately, God does not operate like the world. By giving His life on the cross for you, Jesus Christ took your sins, failures, shortcomings, and removed them from you. The Bible teaches that your sins are as far as the east is from the west. In other words, when Jesus is at home in your heart, your sins are no longer visible to God. Spiritually you are completely free. But here is an important point, we need to learn that whether or not we feel forgiven, we are indeed forgiven. How do you go about embracing God's forgiveness?

1. Confession

So many people struggle with guilt and condemnation. Feelings of guilt and condemnation are a real problem and hinder your acceptance of God's forgiveness. Regardless how you feel, you can speak the authority of God's Word over your life. If you continue to confess God's Word over your feelings, they will lose their authority over you. For example, 1 John 1:9 tells you that if you repent and confess your sins, God is faithful to forgive you.

The next time you ask God to forgive you and you continue to feel guilty, verbalize out-loud, "God forgive me." Then quote 1 John 1:9. The power is in hearing the truth.

2. Conquering guilt and condemnation

Only God's love can truly overcome your feelings of guilt and condemnation. Even when you do not feel like it, trust in God's Word. Choose to trust. Here's is a verse I memorized early in my walk with Christ. Jeremiah 29:11 says, For I know the thoughts and plans that I have for you, says the Lord, thoughts and plans for welfare and peace and not for evil, to give you hope in your final outcome.

Once again, it is about making a choice. If you choose to trust in God's love for you, you will overcome guilt and condemnation. These are spiritual weapons of the devil to keep you down. Do not give in to them. Deal with them. Allow the love of Christ to break these bonds.

3. Continuing to mature

Your faith journey is not a sprint. It is a life-long journey. It is taking each day as a gift, even when it feels like you take two steps forward and three steps backwards. Trust me, I know that feeling. That is the nature of this life. Accept it. It is okay. God is working in every step you take, whether forward or backward. Continue to trust in Him. Never give up.

Here is another verse I learned early in my relationship with Christ. It is found in Romans 12:2 and says, do not conform to the pattern of this world, but be transformed by the renewing of your mind. Then you will be able to test and approve what God's will is–His good, pleasing and perfect will. As our minds are transformed into the image of Christ, our guilt and condemnation become less and less. But here is a caveat. Forgiveness is never easy. There are things you can do to help you, as I have stated above. However, unfortunately, there are numerous obstacles to experiencing forgiveness. Let us review those obstacles.

Obstacles to Forgiveness

Forgiveness Is a Choice

Forgiving someone who has hurt you is challenging. It is important to remember that choosing to forgive someone benefits you first. As I have stated, it is the road to freedom. And freedom from unnecessary emotional and spiritual burdens at the end of life is monumental for experiencing peace. The forgiving process begins with a *choice*. You must come to an emotional place of wanting to choose forgiveness. Many factors can motivate making a choice to forgive, but certain motivations are exacerbated when one knows they are closing in on death. The primary motivation is wanting to fix broken relationships. Any significant social relationship brings two possible outcomes. The significant relationship can bring joy and satisfaction or pain and discourse. This translates into experiencing peace or unrest. Dying is hard enough without making it more difficult with one or more broken significant social relationships. Making a choice to forgive puts you on the road to freedom which increases your chances to experience peace at the end of life.

Refusing to forgive and holding on to grudges creates chronic stressors. If you are unforgiving, you get a burst of the stress hormone cortisol every time you think about the offending event. Remembering and fixating on the harm done to you will cause a rise in blood pressure and put an unnecessary strain on your heart. Over the long run, this can make you more susceptible to disease and an array of health problems. You can see how this makes your end-of-life journey far more complicated. Making a choice to forgive is like choosing to stop smoking after you have been diagnosed with lung cancer. It is a wise choice.

Lack of Humility

Making a choice to forgive is born out of humility. Without humility, making a choice to forgive is unlikely. Humility is an attitude. A person with humility recognizes their own limitations, mistakes, and weaknesses. They refuse to ignore, avoid, or try to deny their shortcomings and deficiencies. In other words, a person with humility is not full of themselves. Without this personal insight, it will be difficult for a person to choose to forgive.

The Bible says, "pride goes before a fall." Regardless of your feelings about the Bible, this is a truthful statement. A person full of pride is a person full of themselves. Consequently, this person is likely to make poor choices regarding forgiveness. It will always be the other person's fault. The prideful person is unable to take any responsibility for the harm done. It is always someone else's fault. This is a dangerous precedent to live by. It will cause only anger and bitterness.

Lack of Vulnerability

One reason that humility is difficult for some people is because it places you in a vulnerable position. Here is how it works. You extend forgiveness to someone, whether they harmed you or there was mutual harm done, but they continue to disrespect you or ignore your reaching out. Eventually you will feel like a doormat. The "doormat effect" is harmful. It can lower your self-esteem and trigger your inner voice telling you how unworthy you are.

Fortunately, your ability to experience forgiveness is not subject to the other person. It is wonderful when both parties accept responsibility and desire forgiveness, but that does not always happen. Forgiveness is about relinquishing your right to get even if you are the harmed party. Releasing your anger, frustration, and bitterness can be accomplished regardless of whether the other person excepts your forgiveness or not. Your extending forgiveness is about you. Yes, you will feel vulnerable, and yes, the other person may reject it, but at this stage this process is about you.

Becoming a doormat is another choice you make. There are circumstances where you need to extend forgiveness, which benefits your emotional, mental, and spiritual well-being, but still choose to remove the other person from your life. Toxic social relationships are detrimental and should be avoided in your life. If the toxic relationship is a family member, clear boundaries should be maintained to limit further harmful behavior. Nevertheless, when you remain vulnerable it allows humility to grow within your heart. A heart for humility is a good preventive for anger, resentment, and bitterness.

Resentment

When you believe that you have been treated unfairly resentment can set it. Resentment is the precursor to anger. Resentment leads to a mental process of reliving the hurt over and over. If you allow the resentment to go unchecked, it can consume you. Once resentment has matured and left unchecked, it will lead to wanting to get even. You desire only revenge.

Resentment is dangerous. We all have likes and dislikes. We all have prejudices and biases toward things and people. Let me give you a personal example. I do not like cigarette smoke. When someone is smoking near me, I will attempt to move away from that person. It is not that I dislike the person, I dislike the behavior. We all have these types of biases. Now, what if the person smoking walks up to me and blows smoke in my face? I would deeply resent that and would consequently resent the person. I have a choice. Do I allow my resentment to turn into anger and the desire to get even, maybe by punching the offender in the nose, or do I take a different approach? If I want to take a different course rather than getting even, like walking away, I have refused to give resentment a hold on my heart. If I allow the engagement to escalate, then resentment can take hold and turn into unchecked anger.

Unchecked Anger

Another obstacle to forgiveness is unchecked anger. Anger that is sustaining and pervasive toward another human being is crippling to the forgiveness process. I am not talking about getting upset from time to time. We all experience brief anger and frustration. Here, I am speaking of a deep and constant resentment toward another. A bitter indignation that wishes harm toward another human being. If something bad happened to them, you would rejoice. This type of anger derails forgiveness.

Then there is the person who is angry at life. Nothing seems to go right. Every day is a struggle. Now I realize we all have bad days. But how you see life has an impact on your ability to forgive. How would you feel if the following scenario happened to you?

> The barista at the coffee house took too long to make your latte and then used low-fat milk, instead of regular, as you ordered. When you finally got the right coffee and drove off in your car, someone cut you off in traffic-making you spill your latte on yourself. All of this happened on your birthday, which your best friend forgot. As a matter of fact, the coffee-stained shirt was a birthday present from this same friend two years ago.

As you read this scenario, you can imagine that a day like this might test whether you are prone to ruminate and be angry, or whether you tend to forgive. Here is the point. If you fail to practice forgiveness in everyday life, it is much harder to extend forgiveness to a particular wrong done to you. Forgiveness is like anything else. The more you practice forgiveness the better you become at extending it. If you do not forgive people for hurts, real or imagined, your life will be filled with anger and spite. You may even spend time plotting and seeking revenge or avoiding people that you really ought to be close with.

Bitterness

The power in resentment, anger, and bitterness is in the sequencing. One builds on the other and becomes more emotionally destructive. A simple resentment can fade quickly. As resentment grows, however, it turns into anger and then morphs into bitterness. It is bitterness that becomes a heart cancer. As with resentment and anger, bitterness left unchecked will in every instance destroy forgiveness. In fact, it is impossible to forgive with bitterness in your heart. They are juxtaposed in process and outcome. If you are bitter toward someone, there is no room left for kindness or compassion.

The overarching reason that bitterness is so insidious is because it takes root in the human heart. I grew up in the southern end of the San Joaquin Valley in California where nutgrass is prolific. Nutgrass spreads by sending out stems (roots) underground which send up shoots that become new plants. The root system is elaborate and difficult to eradicate. Once nutgrass takes hold in a yard, it becomes a constant endeavor to battle it. Bitterness is much the same. If allowed to grow, the root system of bitterness can become extensive. In extreme cases, it can completely take over the human heart, as cancer takes over the body.

Henry's Story

Henry was an 83-year-old male who was a full-time resident in the Village, Rosewood's skilled nursing facility. Henry had been placed on hospice with a diagnosis of pancreatic cancer and less than six months to live. I had known Henry for several years. We enjoyed many conversations about his experiences in Korea and his employment as game warden in the Pacific Northwest. Henry's wife had passed several years before I met him. He had three children all with their own families. His son lived in Bakersfield, CA, but his other son and daughter lived out of state.

Henry was a man's man. Hardened over the years because of setbacks and loss, it was this hard exterior that made relationships difficult for him, particularly with his children. It seems that relational dynamics within a family are the most difficult. This was certainly true for Henry.

He had not spoken to them since his wife died. During the five years since her death, Henry had grown more and more isolated and withdrawn.

Henry had taken a liking to me probably because I was a veteran and we would talk about our military days. He would not talk about the war, but he loved to talk about the crazy things he and his buddies would do. We had both been in the army so we would tell stories and laugh. During one of these story-telling times, I asked Henry if we could talk about his diagnosis and impending death. Henry became quiet and after what seemed to be hours he said, "Sure, I guess so." I asked him if he felt ready to die, and with tears in his eyes he mumbled, "No, not really, I'm afraid." I asked Henry what he was afraid of and he had difficulty putting it into words at first. Then he said, "I wasn't a good person. I loved my wife, but I don't think I was a particularly good husband and I have never really been there for my kids."

Henry had not been a church-going type. As a kid, his parents took him to church occasionally but without any real commitment. He had always felt God was mad at him. Over the next few weeks, I met with Henry and we talked about God, his family, and his feelings of inadequacy. We talked about God's forgiveness and how much He loved him. I explained the Good News about Jesus and His redemptive work on the cross. When I felt he was ready, I asked him if he would like to accept God's forgiveness and accept Jesus into his life. Without hesitation, Henry cried out, "Yes, oh yes." This man who stood 6'2" and still had evidence of being physically strong laid in his hospital bed weeping and thanking God. We continued talking and praying and rejoicing together.

Henry had come a long way spiritually, but he was still terminal and estranged from his children. I knew if Henry was going to die with as much peace as possible, he needed to make things right with his family. Over the next week we talked about forgiveness and reconciliation. Henry understood these concepts regarding God. Now it was time for him to understand the power of healing these concepts could bring with broken relationships. Even if his family continued to reject him, he would die knowing he had tried.

Over the next couple of months, Henry became weaker and weaker. He knew his life was slipping away. He also knew his new home would be heaven. That seemed to bring some peace to Henry. Hospice did a wonderful job of managing his pain and he stayed alert much of the time. But time was running out. I asked Henry if he had reached out to his children and with some hesitation he responded, "No, not yet." I asked him why not and he communicated that he was afraid to. We talked more about it and he finally agreed to call them and ask to see them.

I did not see Henry for about a week, then one day I was walking past his room and happened to look in. As I stood there looking through the door, I saw all these people. Several adults, children, and laughter. I was a bit taken back; I did not expect to see a room full of people. The next day I made it a point to stop by Henry's room. He told me that his entire family had been there, in fact they had stayed in town a few days to visit. Apparently, Henry had called each of his children, told them of his circumstances, and wanted to ask for their forgiveness. They had come to town and visited for three days. According to Henry, he had asked for their forgiveness which they gave. But the most shocking part was they asked Henry to forgive them. He said he never saw that coming. As he was telling me the story, tears were coming down his cheeks. Here was a man who had experienced God's forgiveness and his children's. Even though his body had been ravaged by the disease there was something present that had not been there before. Something in his eyes. As I watched his facial expressions, I realized it was a glimmer of peace.

The power of forgiveness and reconciliation is undeniable. It is worth the journey to find it.

Forgiving Your Enemies

Thomas Szasz is quoted as saying, "The stupid neither forgive or forget; the naïve forgive and forget; the wise forgive but do not forget."

What does a true enemy look like? It is a person who either wants to physically hurt you or who would receive great joy by doing something that would diminish your credibility and integrity. This person would rejoice at your downfall. Simply put, an enemy hates you. They might use expressions like: "I can't stand them," "They make me sick," "I can't stand the sight of them." I sincerely hope you have no individual in your life that you would describe as an enemy. But if you do, and the relationship is important to you, it will serve you well to turn your enemy into a friend. I have said this before, but I am going to say it again. You may live much of your life with this type of relationship and do fine. However, when you are in the last season of your life, reconciliation of this relationship becomes important.

As in most cases, forgiving an enemy begins with you. It goes without saying that this process is not easy. In fact, it is a spiritual process. I believe every human being is born with the capacity to forgive and show compassion. These characteristics are part of your DNA. They can, however, be pushed down so deeply within you they are impossible to find. You begin by softening your heart. This is why I call it a spiritual process. If you are a person of faith in God, you will ask for God's help. He is in the heart-softening business.

The Bible tells us to "love our enemies and to pray for those who persecute us."[30] Turning an enemy into a friend is primarily a matter of prayer, but there are some practical steps you can take.

Remembering forgiveness is a choice, what are the next steps? If you are committed to turning your enemy into a friend, then you need to do the following and be patient. I assure you God is at work.

1. As I stated above, you begin with prayer.

But not just any prayer. It needs to be a prayer of blessing. You need to specifically ask God to bless this person; bless their life, their business, their family, their health. You want God to bless the totality of their lives. Can you see why this is a spiritual process? Without God's help, it is nearly impossible to pray for an enemy in this way. This type of prayer is only between you and God.

2. Be deliberate about privacy.

This is serious business. It is only between you and God. You may need to share this for therapeutic reasons, but only to the person you are in counseling with. They have a duty to keep your secrets. I realize this is not easy. However, your motives must be honest. Not talking with other friends and family about your prayers keeps you off the slippery slope of gossip.

3. Once you commit to praying for them, never stop.

It is seldom the case that once forgiven always forgiven. There are times when your forgiveness needs renewal, particularly if the other party continues to refuse reconciliation. The temptation to become bitter can emerge its monstrous head at any moment. So be diligent. Remain faithful to the process even when you do not feel like it. There are good days and bad days; feelings come and go. You may need to ask God to strengthen you and protect you from negative voices in your heart.

4. Let them see Christ.

When you find yourself around this person, allow them to see Christ within you. In other words, be pleasant and respectful. Keep your composure and treat them as Christ has treated you. Kindness and compassion go a long way. However, make sure to read the section on being a "doormat." You do not need to make them your best friend. Just be Christlike to them.

Let me remind you of the words of Paul in 2 Corinthians 5:19, "God was reconciling the world to himself in Christ, not counting men's sins against them. And he has committed to us the message of reconciliation." Think of praying for your enemies like this, you have been given a privilege to do Christ's work. It is the work of miracles. Be patient, be diligent, and look for God's *fingerprints* on your labor. I promise you will find them.

Dorothy's Story

Dorothy was an eighty-three-year-old female living in the Village. She was small in stature, standing 5 feet 3 inches. However, what she lacked in physical height she made up for in strength of character. Her face clearly showed her age, but her eyes were as bright and clear as any I have seen. She died two months ago. Prior to her passing, I was able to have many conversations with her about her life and her pending death. She professed a strong faith in God but found it exceedingly difficult to accept her death. Twenty years earlier, Dorothy had had both breasts removed and made a full recovery. Until now. The cancer had finally returned and had metastasized throughout her body. She knew she had only several months to live. Dorothy expressed to me on numerous occasions that she was extremely fearful of dying.

As I listened to her and learned more about her story, I was determined to help her experience a peaceful death. We talked about God and her relationship with Him. She seemed to understand God's forgiveness and his love for her. Dorothy had grown up a Catholic but converted to Protestantism during her college days. She told me she was a charismatic in the practice of her faith and attended a Pentecostal church before coming to Rosewood. It was evident she loved the Lord and understood life after death from a Christian perspective.

After hearing about her devotion to Christ and the gospel, I was bewildered about her deep-seated fear of dying. There seemed to be a disconnect, but I was not sure why. As we continued to spend time together, she told me her husband had died several years before and never spoke of children. During all the times I had visited Dorothy, I never saw any family members. I finally asked her one day if she had any children. She became quiet and looked away. When she looked back, I could see tears in her eyes. I asked her if she was okay and she replied, "yes", but not with conviction.

I decided to probe a little deeper. I asked again, "Are you sure you're ok?" She again became quiet and with a quivering lower lip started telling me more of her story. Dorothy had married in her late twenties and had a child nine months later. Her life seemed perfect. She had married the man of her dreams and now had a beautiful baby boy. Dorothy and her husband both graduated from Bible College and were now in the ministry: her husband, a pastor, and she a pastor's wife and another baby on the way. Dorothy described her life as, "grand." Then everything changed. Within a three-month period, she lost her son to an ice-skating accident and experienced a miscarriage. As Dorothy was sharing her story, it became evident that she had never fully recovered from her loss.

As I sat there listening, it became harder and harder to hold back tears. My heart was breaking for her. However, I wanted to press on and understand why after all these years she still felt such grief. As I continued to listen and practice the ministry of presence, it became clear. Dorothy was angry with God, and she believed deeply that God was angry with her. Even though she had expressed a deep faith and love for the Lord, that was more lip-service than true feelings.

As she sat up in her hospital bed with the tears flowing, she asked if she could tell me something that she had never told anyone else. I said, "Yes, of course." For over sixty-years, Dorothy explained, she had been so angry with God that she hated him. Moreover, it was obvious to Dorothy that God hated her because he allowed both of her children to perish. There had been no forgiveness and reconciliation on Dorothy's part. Consequently, she believed her rejection of God placed her under his damnation. According to Dorothy, she would go to hell and never see her children in heaven. As I heard these words, I knew why Dorothy was so afraid to die.

Over the next several weeks as Dorothy became weaker, we talked about the importance of forgiveness and reconciliation: concepts she only knew in her head. I once heard the phrase, "death is the great equalizer." As Dorothy and I talked candidly about her death, she began to realize she did not want to die with such guilt and fear. Dorothy had plenty of religious training, but this was an issue of the heart. She knew she needed to soften her heart towards God. During one of our last conversations, I told Dorothy she needed heart surgery. Spiritual heart surgery. I kindly, but directly, told her if she wanted to die peacefully, she would need to experience forgiveness and reconciliation. First, for herself. She needed to forgive herself for being angry with God for the loss of her children. Second, she needed to accept God's forgiveness, then she could experience reconciliation and God's peace. I told her this process would lead to a sense of thankfulness and a readiness to meet her children in heaven. Through tears and prayers, she did just that.

I went into her room the next day. When my image caught her sight, she blessed me with a slight smile. Eyes still as clear and bright as ever. As I moved closer to her bed, she motioned for me to come closer, as if she wanted to say something. At this point, Dorothy had only hours to live. When I bent over and placed my ear close to her mouth, she whispered, "I'm ready." As I stood up, her smile got bigger. Her whole face seemed brighter. I was about to ask her what she was ready for; then I realized she had found the peace that had been elusive.

Several days after Dorothy passed, I was given a note. It was from Dorothy. The handwriting was difficult to read but was filled with a joyous tone. She thanked me for taking the time to talk with her about forgiveness. She told me I had been right. Forgiveness does lead to reconciliation and being reconciled leads to gratitude. The note said she was thankful for me and for God's love; that she was no longer afraid to die. As I continued to read her note tears filled my eyes. Dorothy did not know it, but she left me a wonderful legacy. A legacy of how to die well.

Preparing for a Good Death

Most people have unfinished business. Generally, this unfinished business falls into three categories:

1. They carry emotional wounds resulting in regrets and they want forgiveness.
2. They want to be remembered by the people who are important in their lives.
3. They want to know their life mattered.

I have often said that people die as they have lived. If you want to die well, meaning experiencing peace at the end, you need to live as if today is your last. If you have lived by the principles of forgiveness, reconciliation, and gratitude, you probably feel ready. Unfortunately, most people do not live this way throughout life. We have lingering broken relationships that have not been reconciled. We wonder if people with whom we are estranged will be glad when we are gone. Brokenness leads to feeling that one's life never mattered. This is a terrible way to die.

If you fall into the above group, you may be feeling despair. But take heart; I have wonderful news. It is never too late. Mending significant social relationships in preparation for death is the road to freedom and peace. Ira Byock is a hospice doctor who wrote, *The Four Things that Matter Most.* In his book he gives us four important phrases, "Please forgive me. I forgive you. Thank you. I love you." Forgiveness, reconciliation, and gratitude carry enormous power to mend a wide range of social relationships. But you cannot wait for someone else to reach out. You must reach out and begin the journey of preparing for the inevitable end of life. You can never start too early. Remember the phrase, "you die as you have lived."

For over a decade I have worked in a senior living community serving what Tom Brokaw called the greatest generation. In fact, he wrote a marvelous book by the same name. If you have never read it, I would recommend it. During my tenure working specifically with seniors, I have had the privilege to perform over three hundred funerals. I sat by the side of many of these seniors as they passed. What a great privilege that is! There is one individual whose story is unique, unique because she embodied every aspect of dying well.

Every other weekend I volunteered as an emergency room chaplain in our county hospital. It was a busy hospital on Friday and Saturday nights. We took most of the gunshots, stabbings, car wrecks, drug overdose, and victims of violence. The emergency room had twenty-five beds that were generally full on any given weekend. I met Josephine in one of those beds. She was an eighty-six old female I met after she was admitted to the emergency room for being struck in a crosswalk by a hit-and-run driver. Fortunately, her injuries were not life-threatening, and she was discharged the next day. However, during the evening I had the honor to get to know Josephine. She was a remarkable lady.

Josephine's Story

She lived in the house that she and her husband purchased shortly after he returned from the war. They had been married 63 years prior to his death. As we talked that evening about life and death, I was enchanted by her story. I wanted to hear more. As I sat with her, I learned two things about Josephine that intrigued me. First, she was dying of cancer. Second, her optimistic and upbeat attitude was contagious. I told Josephine I was doing research on how people die and asked if I could interview her over the next couple of weeks. A big smile crossed her face, and she replied, "Of course you can, I would enjoy the company."

We met once a week for three weeks. I had never met a more positive person. It was not because her life had been easy. Quite the contrary. Josephine grew up extremely poor in Oklahoma. Her father had been a mechanic and her mother washed clothes for other people. She did not learn to read and write until she was in sixth grade. She never went to high school. She told me in those days, girls were not really expected to go beyond the eighth grade. After finishing her schooling, Josephine worked with her mother. She made twenty-five cents a day. That money went to help pay for family bills. When she was sixteen, Josephine started working as a maid for a wealthy family across town. She walked three miles one way to her job.

As I listened to Josephine's story, week after week, I could not help but feel privileged to know her. She was small in stature, only about 5' 2", but her heart was huge. Her hair was grey, her complexion was weathered by time, but her eyes were bright blue and sparkling. If you only saw her eyes, you would think she was twenty years old. It was remarkable. No doubt she had been attractive in her earlier years.

Josephine got married when she was twenty. Late for girls in the 1940s. She met Thomas, who would become her husband, at a barn dance during the war. Thomas had been home on leave from the navy. They had four children, however her first was still born. They never had a lot of money, but Josephine said their lives were full. I asked her in what way. She stated, "because I was always grateful." Her comment interested me. I asked her to explain. Josephine said with a smile, "throughout my life I have always been thankful for everything I had. My husband, my family, my life." "Even during the difficult times, I was grateful. I felt like the life I had been given was a gift and I should make the best of it." I told her it sounded like a fairytale. She quickly commented, "Oh no, it was never a fairytale, mostly it was hard." "I lost a child, two grandchildren, and my husband suffered for years with dementia." She went on to say that her life had never been easy.

As our interview continued over several weeks, I discovered Josephine had carried tremendous guilt over the loss of her first born. Besides her guilt, she never understood why God would allow two of her grandchildren to die so early in life. A boy had drowned while swimming in a lake and a girl had been thrown from a horse breaking her neck. Both tragedies had left Josephine severely shaken in her faith that God was good. As we talked, Josephine started to cry. Tears were running down her cheeks and her voice was breaking. I was beginning to feel how difficult her life had been and the depth of her pain.

During our last interview I asked Josephine how she got through all the hardships she had experienced throughout life. She quickly said, "I found redemption." I said, "really? How did that happen?" Josephine spent the next three hours telling me about her struggle to overcome her feelings of guilt and pain.

Josephine explained she had stopped praying years before. Then just after her husband's death, she went on a trip with her son and his family. Her son thought it would be good for her to get away, so he took her on a cruise. She had never been on one and was reluctant to go. But her son persuaded her, and they left for a seven-day cruise around the northern Caribbean. She had always loved the ocean but felt empty inside and was not looking forward to leaving her home.

As Josephine was telling me her story, I noticed a glimmer in her eyes that I had not seen since our first interview three weeks earlier. According to Josephine, they were somewhere near Anguilla and she was standing on the deck watching the sunset and all of sudden she felt God's presence. As I listened, I saw her eyes twinkle and the joy in her face as she shared her experience. The beauty of this moment, she said, "reminded my heart that God was faithful and had always been there." In that moment, Josephine said, "she felt God's forgiveness and his peace." She went on to say, "I can't really explain it, except in that moment I was able to forgive myself and accept his forgiveness." She continued, "it was the oddest experience, but in a really good way." "It made me feel whole."

I was mesmerized listening to her. Josephine had lived in that forgiveness ever since. That is why when she received the diagnosis of stage IV bone cancer that had metastasized, she had peace. Doctors had given her less than six months to live. As Josephine was telling me about the last six months and her battle, my eyes started to get misty. Then something happened I will never forget. Josephine reached out with her tiny hand and touched my face and smiled. She said, "Terry, don't cry for me, don't even be sad. I am the happiest I have ever been. I'm at complete peace and ready to go." As I looked into her eyes, I could see the truth of her statement. She was indeed at peace.

Josephine passed three weeks later. Her funeral was truly a celebration of life. As I sat listening to the pastor, all I could think about was the healing power that forgiveness, reconciliation, and gratitude brings. Josephine was a poster child for all three.

We Die as We Have Lived

Every once in a while, you come across people that change your life. Josephine was one of those people. The longer I live, the more convinced I am that how you choose to live in the present, determines how you will leave this life. It is really your choice. You can choose to live your life in regrets and bitterness, or in forgiveness and reconciliation. Whichever way you choose will determine your end game. Your goal should not be a good death. Your goal should be a good life. If you live life well, you will die well.

In *Finishing Well to the Glory of God*, John Dunlop, MD writes, "If we recognize that we are slowly dying, we have a window of opportunity to make the best of the waning days of our lives. We will no longer be worried about how we will die or even when. We can simply accept it and determine to live each day well so that when the time comes, we will be ready."[31] Researchers report that 39 percent of terminally ill patients indicated that strengthening family relationships was one of their major priorities.[32]

I encourage you to live like today is your last day. Live in the power of forgiveness. If you are willing to walk this journey, you will see every day as a gift. A precious gift. And death becomes your final act of love. The way you die will be your legacy to the living. You become a guide for all who knew you. What a wonderful way to leave this life.

Chapter Eight

RECONCILIATION

"True reconciliation is never cheap, for it is based on forgiveness which is costly."

~ Desmond Tutu

Many people think that reconciliation means forgiveness. There is, however, a significant difference. You can experience forgiveness without reconciliation. You cannot experience reconciliation without forgiveness. Reconciliation is the observable healing behavior that flows from forgiveness and is equally as important as forgiveness. Reconciliation—the dictionary definition is to restore friendship or harmony or to settle or resolve differences— transforms both parties by bringing them to a new consciousness about the way they see, treat, and represent each other.

Reconciliation is a discipline that takes work to develop. Why it takes work is because it does not always come easily. It requires a strong level of commitment. When you have a broken social relationship and it is a significant relationship, then repairing the relationship (if possible) is important. It is particularly important at the end of life. Here are several examples when reconciliation is not practical or necessary.

When reconciliation is not necessary.

Let me introduce you to Judy. I first met Judy when I worked for a non-profit in my hometown. Judy was one of those people that just drew you in as you talked with her. When you were in her presence, she made you feel like you were the only person in the world. As we served on the board of directors together, I got to know Judy's story. More specifically, the story about her relationship with her father. Judy had been estranged from her father for many years. There had been some sort of breakdown of their relationship; however, she did not elaborate. What she did share with me was that the relationship had been restored to a degree. Judy lived in California and her father lived in Michigan, so the level of restoration took place over the phone. The restoration involved both parties saying how sorry they were for the broken relationship. Both asked the other to forgive their part in the hurt. Forgiveness was asked for and given. Judy described this moment as transforming.

Several months later, before they could see each other, Judy's father died. Judy was grateful for the healing words that had been shared between them. It made all the difference in the world, according to Judy. But there was something still missing. There had been no physical reconciliation. There had been emotional healing, but no living out the forgiveness that had been expressed. This left Judy feeling less than whole. The forgiveness and reconciliation process had not been completed. You might think of it like this. It is a hot day and you are extremely thirsty. Someone hands you a glass of lukewarm water. You are grateful for the water, but if there were ice cubes in the glass, it would be amazingly refreshing. Judy was thankful for the forgiveness but missed having time to live that forgiveness out.

Now let me introduce Jeff. Jeff is a middle-aged man, married to a wonderful woman of twenty-two years of age. He and his wife have two children they both adore. Their marriage is solid, and they are each other's best friend. But like most marriages, there are moments when trust gets broken. Jeff considers himself to be a man of integrity and generally follows through on his promises. However, from time to time he drops the ball, not because he does not care, but because he gets distracted.

Jeff is a lawyer and his job is stressful. There are many deadlines to meet and details that require his complete focus. There have been several times when his focus caused problems. Several weeks ago, Jeff and I were having lunch. We had been talking about our lives and he shared this story. Jeff's oldest son was a junior in high school. He was also a varsity basketball player. It was the last game of the season and would determine which team would go to the state championships. Jeff had promised his son that he would be at the game. It was Friday afternoon and Jeff had three briefs that needed to be filed with the court prior to end of business. He was running late and completely forgot about his son's game until the fourth quarter. When Jeff arrived at the gym, there were only four minutes left in the game. He felt terrible. Jeff had not missed a game all year. When the game was over, Jeff went up to his son, and apologized for being so late. He even asked his son to forgive him, which his son did without hesitation.

In this situation, depending on the relationship that had been established, forgiveness will generally restore the relationship. Reconciliation is part and parcel with forgiveness. Minor infractions that happen within an otherwise strong relationship do not need proof of reconciliation. Forgiveness will heal the wound. These infractions must be infrequent and not the normal behavior. If minor infractions happen over and over, they become the norm. Over the course of time, minor infractions can become major hurts. When this line is crossed, complete forgiveness and full reconciliation will be the only way to heal the hurt. This can only be achieved with changed behavior. The changed behavior must be lived out consistently over time.

When reconciliation leads to restoration.

With the examples above, you probably sense the "degree" of brokenness is important. In most cases where a significant social relationship has been damaged, both forgiveness and reconciliation are necessary. As I have stated earlier, these two concepts become more important at the end of life. Remember, every emotion and spiritual need is exacerbated during the last season of life. The importance of some things falls away, while other things become far more important. Significant social relationships are at the top of the list of important things.

Practicing Reconciliation

Maybe you have heard of the five Ws and the H in research. The Who, What, When, Where, and Why questions must be answered, along with the How in covering all the bases in any research project. I want you to think of practicing reconciliation as a project. A project that you will work on the rest of your life. Think of this project as part of being human. We all make mistakes. We all get hurt and hurt others. So, practicing reconciliation is something you will do your entire life, or at least you should. Remember what I said about dying well, "if you want to die well, you need to live well." One way we live well is to practice forgiveness and reconciliation. Walk through the five Ws and H with me. Ask these questions for yourself.

Who:

This should be obvious and self-evident. Any stakeholder in a significant social relationship is the "who." If you are one of these individuals, then you probably know when a relationship is not right. There is a brokenness. A feeling that a chasm between you and the other person is present and getting deeper. Whenever you think of this individual, there is an uneasiness within you. You are not at peace with this person. I talked about humility and vulnerability in Chapter One. These are important concepts to understand and internalize. You will need to practice both, moving forward if you desire restoration. This will take courage. I hope as you read this book you will find the necessary courage to take the necessary steps to heal the relationship.

What:

This question deals with what you are trying to accomplish. On the surface it may seem obvious, but let me flush it out, so you and I have the same understanding. By reaching out to offer forgiveness and hopefully reconciliation, you are attempting to heal hurts that reduce your ability to communicate. Without communication, all relationships suffer and fail over time. Working towards restoring a relationship is working towards holding that person in esteem, rather than in negativity. When this is accomplished, your heart begins to soften, allowing you to begin releasing the hurt. Think of your life as the palm of a hand. You can either close your hands into a tight fist or open your hands with palms up. The closed tight fist represents a closed-off life emotionally. Open hands represent a willingness to live in freedom and refusing to live in negativity.

One way to live with open hands is to realize that you are not always right. You need to examine your situation with a heart open to the possibility the other person has good reason to feel the way they do. This is where a sense of humility comes in. You may determine that your position is absolutely right. Even if it is, you still need to attempt to repair the relationship. If you wait for the other person, it may never happen. Reach out! You have nothing to lose and everything to gain. Even if the other person refuses to engage with you, you tried. The Bible declares the following, "Do all that you can to live in peace with everyone."[33] Knowing that you tried to mend a broken relationship will bring peace.

When:

When should you reach out to the other person? Every situation is different. Maybe you have been estranged from a significant relationship for many years, or maybe it just happened. Either way, the time is now. If you are reading this book, something in your heart is telling you it is time. In the human experience, reconciliation usually comes after interpersonal conflict. You are torn inside. You want to fix the relationship, but you feel you need justice. And the justice you seek is for the other person to acknowledge their wrongdoing by coming to you first. Unfortunately, waiting for your perceived justice may never come. If you have been given a short time to live, the "when" becomes important. If you want peace as you face death, do not wait for someone else to initiate.

You have heard the phrase, "It is never too late." Generally, I believe that. However, if you have been diagnosed with a terminal illness, there is a point of no return. You could become incapacitated or die. Either way, your window of opportunity will pass. More importantly, you have suffered all the way to the end. Do not allow this to happen.

Where:

I would encourage you to meet with the person face to face in a quiet moment. Meet in a place that is non-threatening. A restaurant, park, or a coffee house can be a good choice. You are the best judge regarding this question. You know the other person. I encourage you to listen to your heart. You will know the right time and place. Although face to face is the best way to meet, you could also call, text, or email. While these are not ideal, it does show initiative and gives the other person a chance to respond. You could also write a letter. A letter can be an effective way to communicate. Think about what you want to say. Read it several times. Rewrite it if necessary. This form of communication gives you ample time to say exactly what you intend. Even if you are meeting face to face, it is a good idea to write out what you plan to say.

Why:

As you read this book, the "why" question should be self-evident. When people discover that the end of life is near, everything takes on a different perspective. As I have said, the most important aspect of living and knowing your time is coming to an end, are significant social relationships. It is impossible to feel ready to die with broken relationships. You will not be thinking, "I wish I could have worked more, or I had more stuff." These notions fall away, and you are left with relationships as priorities.

Reconciliation, whether it is between you and another human being or between you and God, it is the road to freedom. For you to die with peace, you need freedom. Freedom from the burdens of guilt, shame, anger, and bitterness. Without freedom from these feelings, you will never feel ready to pass from this life. And pass you will. So, my sincere hope is that you take my words to heart. Restore what is broken. It will make all the difference.

How:

The "how" question is the overarching process that brings everything together. The "how" question moves you from an academic exercise to a behavioral commitment. This is the execution of the five Ws. You have heard the phrase, "This is where the rubber meets the road." Your road to forgiveness and reconciliation is about to take shape. So, how do you begin? Here is a list of ten ways to help your rubber meet the road.

1. **Pen and paper**: I want you to think about all the people with whom you need to reconcile. It may be only one, or it may be several. Whatever the number, write their names in a journal or on a piece of paper. It is important to get the process out of your head and into a tangible format. This will help you stay focused, particularly if there are numerous names.

You might consider having to two columns. One column for the people you have reached out to and the other column for the ones you still need too. Make journal entries as things progress. Under each name write out your steps to reconcile and their responses. Forgiveness and reconciliation are a fluid process. With some relationships, it may take time. Journaling will help you stay focused and determined.

2. **Monitor your heart's focus**: As I have stated, forgiveness and reconciliation are a spiritual process, therefore motives must be authentic. It will be important for you to do a self-assessment from time to time. This is particularly important with difficult relationships. Make sure you understand the feelings that are motivating you. This process is not about revenge or getting even. It is about forgiveness and reconciliation. I keep repeating it, because with difficult relationships it is easy to become sidetracked. Be honest with yourself.

3. **Be willing to let go**: This is where vulnerability and humility come in. I would never suggest this is an easy process. It is not. Nevertheless, it is vital to accomplishing your goal. You may need to redirect your attention from the hurt, frustration, anger, and guilt you have suffered, to a place of conversation. Forgiveness and reconciliation will never be achieved without conversation. These issues must be talked out.

Letting go of past hurts is a choice. This does not make you weak. In fact, it makes you strong. It will make you stronger emotionally. It also brings clarity. Clarity for you to see the bigger picture of forgiveness and reconciliation. When you choose to let go of certain hurts, you are choosing forgiveness. This choice can lead you into a conversation with the other person that can change both of your lives. I am not suggesting you forget the hurt. I am asking that you set it aside so you can move forward.

4. **Deciding on the conversation**: I have mentioned above that forgiveness and reconciliation will be elusive until there is a conversation. This may seem obvious, but this particular conversation is often complicated and difficult. The other person is likely to have negative feelings towards you. Normally, this type of encounter would make you defensive. Therefore, it feels emotionally risky. It is also why step 3 above is important. Getting defensive will only sabotage the conversation.

I encourage you to begin this conversation with only a few pre-conceived ideas. Attempt to maintain an openness. You may think you have the only solution but keep your heart open for different possibilities. You might discover your conversation turns into a negation. Be open to finding solutions together.

5. **Role-play with a friend**: You may think this sounds like child's play, but it can be an effective way to prepare for the conversation with the other person. Have a trusted friend play the other person. Walk through the conversation. This will help you understand the other person's position and help clarify yours. When I was in law school and preparing for a Moot Court competition, I used this technique. It proved to be immensely helpful. Make it as real as possible. Keep in mind your motives and intentions for the conversation. Once again, it is not about getting even. It is about finding common ground resulting in reconciliation of the relationship.

6. **Having "the" conversation**: I realize that every situation is different. Depending on the issues and the depth of hurt, will dictate the substance of the conversation. Sometimes it is possible to restore the relationship without going over the actual causes of the hurt. If issues do not need to be discussed, then leave them be. Focus on what is necessary to restore the relationship. Try to leave nothing of importance out, but resist bringing up old baggage if not necessary.

You must remember this will be a difficult conversation. But also remember, nothing of value is ever easy. The difficulty of this process will be well worth it. Know what you want to say and say it with grace. Stay calm. Take a breath and refuse to allow your emotions to get out of control. If you need a break, take it. If you need to come back another day, schedule it. Remember, this is a "process."

7. **Follow through**: Once you and the other person have reached common ground and hopefully a clear understanding, you are ready for the next step. This is where the "promise" is made. Putting it into legal language, this is where you and the other person enter a contract. You both need to commit to making a change in the relationship. Even though this does not always happen, it is ideal. Here are some points of the contractual arrangement:

> a. Because negativity and gossip can be so destructive, promise each other that you will refrain from being critical of the other. You will not speak in negative terms about the other.

> b. If other issues arise, promise to bring them to the table. But it is not a communal table. It is a private table. Issues are discussed privately and only with the other person.

> c. As I said, this is a process. You may need to agree to disagree on some issues. If that need arises, do it with respect and integrity.

> d. If you reach an impasse, do not panic, take a breath, and come back to the issue later. Ultimately, to save the relationship this may be an issue you will need to agree to disagree about. If you have practiced "letting go" you will be able to do this.

8. **Remembering the past**: I am sure you have watched court dramas on television or in movies. Once the attorneys have presented their cases, each attorney has the right to make a closing argument or statement. I encourage you to pull out your journal and write a closing statement. You want a reminder to leave the brokenness of this relationship in the past. What is in the past must stay there. Do not bring it up again. Never use it in a moment of frustration. This statement is only for you. No one else needs to see it. It is your reminder of the process for forgiveness and reconciliation.

I do, however, want you to remember the past. You do not need to try and forget. I call this *forgiveness with remembrance*. When you remember, you are less likely to repeat your mistakes. Do not be afraid to remember. Remembering the past will help you to appreciate the value of reconciliation.

9. **When the conversation fails:** Since you have no control over the other person, they may or may not receive your desire for forgiveness and reconciliation. If no common ground is found and you are unable to bridge your differences, there are several things you can do. First, re-examine your position. Is there anywhere you were not clear? Did the other person misunderstand you on some point? Were you too demanding in your position? This self-evaluation can be difficult but important. Be honest with yourself. Could you have tried harder? This leads me to step 10.

10. **Be prayerful**: This whole process must be covered in prayer. Forgiveness and reconciliation are about the heart. Prayer is about the heart. The concepts of forgiveness and reconciliation are bigger than you and the other person. When they are released, they are powerful and dynamic. They embody the very nature of God. Therefore, to exclude God from the process can severely hinder the work of forgiveness and reconciliation. God is the author of both. I have talked a lot about the power of forgiveness and reconciliation.

I have seen it displayed in my life and countless others. It is my conviction that human beings are created with the capacity to forgive and be reconciled. The Bible tells us that we are created in God's image. I believe this to mean that human beings have similar capacities as God has, specifically to forgive and to be reconciled. Whether you believe in God or not, you have these capacities. Prayer is the glue that holds these concepts together and empowers them in our lives.

Janet's Story

One winter day in 2016 I was doing rounds in our skilled nursing facility. I happened to walk past a room on the east wing and heard someone crying. I knocked and walked into the room and saw a woman in the bed next to the window, sobbing. I slowly walked over to her bed, put my hand her shoulder and asked if she was okay. Then I introduced myself and told her I was the chaplain. I do not think she even knew I was there. Her crying was making it hard for her to breathe. As her eyes opened and she looked up at me, I asked again, are you okay. As she closed her eyes again, seconds passed. I spoke again, "Janet, can you tell me why you are upset?" Her eyes opened and her crying slowed. She looked at me and replied, "I'm not ready to die."

As I stood next to Janet, she turned away from me and looked out the window. She was still crying but not as hard. I asked her if I could pray with her. She responded, "I don't think that's going to help." Janet was a new arrival. She had been in the skilled nursing facility for just over a week. Consequently, I did not know much about her background. I continued to engage her with small talk and she finally stop crying. As I asked questions trying to get to know her, I finally asked if she was a religious person. She paused for a moment, then stated, "No, not really. I'm not sure I even believe in a God." We talked further about what brought her to skilled nursing. Several weeks prior, Janet had fallen in her home and broken her hip. She spent three or four days in the hospital, then came to skilled nursing for rehabilitation. She was not happy about being there. She mentioned that fact numerous times during our conversation. I could tell she was getting tired. I asked her if I could drop by and visit again tomorrow and she gave me a nod and said, "yes."

The next morning, I stopped by Janet's room, but her bed was empty. I assumed she had been taken to our rehab department for exercises. I made a mental note to return later in the day. That afternoon I returned around 3:00 clock. Janet was lying in her bed drinking some juice. I knocked and walked in. As I approached her bed, I said, "Hi Janet, how are you feeling today?" I noticed she was not crying. She looked at me and responded, "I'm OK, I guess." We spent the next thirty minutes talking about nothing important, just more small talk. I was beginning to feel that Janet was just tolerating my presence. She did not seem to be in the mood to talk about anything of substance. I once again excused myself and left her room.

It was several days before I got back to see Janet. As I walked in, she was having lunch. She seemed to have a good appetite. This was my third visit and I was hoping we could get beyond the small talk. I wanted to know why Janet was afraid to die. After a few pleasantries, I sat down next to her bed and asked if I could ask a question. She looked at me with an inquisitive look and said, "yes, of course." Sensing Janet was in a better mood, I decided to ask her the question that had been on my heart. I began, "Janet, the other day you told me you were afraid to die. Can you tell me why you are afraid?" Tears began to form in her eyes and her lower lip was quivering. At that moment, I thought Janet was about to refuse my request. Then all of sudden, she looked at me and said, "yes, I would, actually."

Janet started by saying, "I'm eighty years old and have seen much of life, more than I care to remember. Several months before I fell and ended up here, I was diagnosed with terminal cancer. They gave me 12 to 24 months to live. That news hit me like a freight train. I could not believe it. I'm just not ready." With that statement, Janet's eyes began to tear up. I asked her, "can you tell me why you don't feel ready?" She found some composure and shared the following story.

Janet had gotten married at the age of 23. She and her husband were living in Wisconsin at the time. They had been married several years when Janet became pregnant. Life was good until one day. As Janet was telling me about those early years, I sensed a tragedy brewing. With tears she continued. It was a beautiful Sunday afternoon in early December. The air was crisp, without a cloud in the sky. Janet and her husband and daughter went to church in the morning, came home and had lunch. It was the family custom to attend a Sunday evening service. Church had been an important part of their lives. On this particular Sunday evening, Janet did not feel up to going back to church. She had worked all afternoon cooking and in her garden. So, she decided to stay home to rest. Her husband needed to get some work done for Monday morning and decided not to go as well. Rachel, their daughter who was a junior in high school was active in the high school program at church. Over the last month, Rachel had been rehearsing a part in the church play. She would play Mary when the play opened in two weeks.

Since Rachel's parents had decided not to go to church, a friend of Rachel's had agreed to pick her up and drive her. Her friend was a senior and had been driving for over a year. Janet knew the young lad and trusted him. On the way to the church, a drunk driver ran a stop sign and hit the two broadside. The impact was on Rachel's side, who was killed instantly. Her friend survived but sustained major injuries. The driver who hit them was not injured. As I sat there listening to Janet tell her story, my heart was breaking. I could only imagine the pain that Janet and her husband endured. But I still was not clear on why Janet was so afraid of death. In my experience there were always specific reasons, and I wanted to know.

Janet paused with her story and took a drink of water. She had stopped crying, but tears were still present in her eyes. I knew by sharing this story, Janet was reliving every terrible moment. I was not sure I should press any further, but I still felt compelled to ask about her fear. As I was about to ask another question, Janet said she was tired and wanted to rest. I told her I completely understood and asked if I could return later in the week. She said, "yes of course." Then she said, "I haven't talked about Rachel's death for 30 years. My husband passed three years ago, but we never talked about it." I leaned over and gently kissed her on the forehead and said goodbye.

Our last conversation had been on a Wednesday. I had hoped to see Janet again on Friday, but was unable to because of another emergency. Monday morning, I had arrived at work early for a meeting. My meeting ended at 10:30 and I went directly to Janet's room. I had thought about her story all weekend. I was not sure why, but I had been deeply disturbed by the events Janet had lived through. I was even more convinced I needed to know why she was fearful of dying. I was sure it had something to do with her daughter.

When I walked into the room, Janet was asleep. I decided not to wake her and turned to leave. As I approached the door, I heard, "chaplain, come back." I turned around and was greeted with a sleepy smile. Janet told me not to leave but come in and have a seat. I walked over to her bed and sat down. We exchanged words of greeting, and then I asked how she was feeling. She replied, "fairly good today. This is my day off from the rehab, so I was napping." I told her napping was good and we both smiled. As we settled into each other's company, I decided to ask her the question about her fear again. I reached over and took her hand and said, "Janet," do you feel like talking about your fear of death this morning?" She quietly said, "yes, I guess so."

With all the gentleness I could muster, I asked her about the fear she had about dying. "Janet" I said, "why do you think you're so afraid of dying?" She looked at me with apprehension in her eyes and said,

"I feel so guilty. I should have taken Rachel to church that night. If I had, she might still be alive. I have lived with this guilt for over 50 years. I hate myself for causing my daughter's death. And I hate God for allowing her to die." As I sat there speechless, it felt like time had stopped. Janet continued, "I have tried to find peace and forgiveness, but I don't think I deserve it. I am a wretched person. I know God has abandoned me." "For the first few years after the accident I prayed for redemption, but it never came." Then Janet started to cry loudly, painfully. The depth of her pain was unimaginable. I asked her again if I could pray for her. She looked at me and through the tears said, "No!" The tone in her voice made the hair standup on the back of my neck. I could almost see the pain go from bitterness to anger and back again. As I left, I told her I would pray for her. She turned her head and gazed out the window.

For the next couple of days, I could not get Janet off my mind. I had no idea how I was going to help her, or even if I could. She was closed off to anything spiritual. She had lived this way so long, it almost seemed normal to her. But the time was fast approaching when things would begin to change. Janet was dying. She would be leaving the skilled nursing facility in a few weeks and I might never see her again. I was carrying a burden for Janet I could not explain. Then it hit me. It was self-forgiveness. It was the very thing I had experienced with my father. In my case, it was ten years I carried such guilt and shame. Janet had been carrying it for almost six decades.

A week had passed before I visited Janet again. This was intentional; I could not go back until I had something to say. So, I prayed. I prayed for a week, specifically about how to help Janet. It was Sunday evening (looking back, I found that to be interesting), and I was saying my prayers before I went to bed. I felt impressed to tell Janet my story about my father. The next morning, I went to see Janet. The staff was packing her things. She was sitting in a wheelchair next to the bed. I said good morning and asked Janet if she was leaving.

She looked at me without any expression and said, "yea, I'm going home. My doctor thinks I've had enough rehab because the cancer is progressing faster than they expected." I must have looked confused because she asked me, "you OK, chaplain?" She had never once called me by my first name. I responded, "yea…um, yes, I'm fine." As the two nursing assistants finished packing Janet's belongings, I asked Janet if we could have lunch together before she left? I pushed her into the main dining room and sat down. Janet was across from me. There was no one else at our table.

Once the food was brought to our table and we started to eat, I told Janet that I had a story to tell her. A personal story. With little expression, she said, "Oh really. Well okay." I told her about how I had left my father, basically to die in an assisted living facility. And for ten years I carried such guilt and shame because of my selfishness, it was difficult to bear. Then one day I felt the Lord's presence and my guilt and shame was lifted. Over the next 45 minutes, I shared the entire story with her. She seemed genuinely interested but showed little emotion. We finished lunch, exchanged pleasantries once again, and said goodbye.

To be honest, I was disappointed. I was sure that God was going to do something awesome in Janet's life. As I watched her being wheeled out to the parking lot, I felt a sense of failure. I said a short, silent prayer for Janet then returned to my office. Several weeks went by and I thought less and less about Janet. My days were full of counseling, Bible studies, visitations, and meetings. As time went on, I seldom remembered my time with Janet. Then one day about a month later I got a call on my cell phone. It was a Sunday evening and I was relaxing at home when my phone rang. I did not recognize the number and almost deleted the call, but something inside me compelled me to answer.

I said hello and heard Janet's voice. She sounded excited and out of breath. As I listened, I could not make out what she was saying. I asked her to calm down and tell me what was wrong. There was a pause, then Janet said, "chaplain Terry, nothing is wrong. Everything is right." I replied, "What? What do you mean Janet?" She continued, "I know Jesus loves me. I feel His joy with me." Now I was speechless. I asked, "Wow, seriously! Tell me what happened." Janet started to explain. Several times I had to slow her down because I could not understand her through the excitement. She stated that over the last month she had thought about my story. She slowly started to pray and ask God to forgive her. The days passed but nothing happened. She still felt guilty and ashamed. She hated herself and her life.

According to Janet, she was walking into her bedroom and caught her foot on a throw rug. She tripped but grabbed the side of her bed which broke her fall. As she sat on the floor crying and alone, she felt God's presence. She described it as overwhelming. A warm sensation came over her and she immediately felt peace. As she continued to explain her encounter with God, I could sense authenticity in her voice. Something incredibly special had happened to Janet. And I knew exactly what that was. She had encountered the risen Lord Jesus. The presence she felt was Jesus Christ, through the power of the Holy Spirit. Instantly, all the guilt, shame, and bitterness had left her. When she accepted Christ's forgiveness, she was able to forgive herself. Fifty years of suffering evaporated. Janet was free.

When I hung up the phone, my heart was full of thankfulness for God's mercy. I began to worship in my spirit, thanking Jesus for saving Janet from suffering. Six months had passed, when I saw an obituary in the paper stating that Janet had died peacefully in her home. I smiled and rejoiced. I knew Janet was home with her family.

Reconciliation in Summary

When I think about Janet and so many others, I am reminded of the power of forgiveness and reconciliation. Whether you are a Christian or not, you have been created with the capacity to forgive. With forgiveness comes reconciliation. When these two concepts become a reality in your life, the reality of your life changes. Remember, to live in the bondage of anger, bitterness, frustration, guilt, and shame is a choice. You can choose differently. There is freedom from this bondage. Put into practice what I have described in this book, and your life will change. Living in this freedom brings peace. It will also bring a sense of readiness when life is drawing short. I have said on several occasions, "you die as you have lived." Living well will help you die well. Dying well is the greatest gift you can give to your loved ones.

In Summary:

Do the following:

- Refuse to deny the problem. Face it with courage and integrity.
- Refuse to stay silent. Allow yourself to be vulnerable with humility.
- Refuse to justify your actions. Seldom are you always right.
- Refuse to complain about the other person.
- Refuse to entertain constant negative thinking about the other person.
- Refuse to engage in ongoing arguments.

Assert the following:

- I will be willing to communicate with the other person.
- I will be willing to shift my attitude from judging and defending to listening.
- I will be willing to empathize with the other person.
- I will be willing to focus on personal growth and learning.

- I will be willing to believe the other person wants reconciliation.
- I will be willing to desire the best for the other person rather than harm.
- I will be willing to hold myself accountable for the process of reconciliation.

In the 1989 movie, Indiana Jones and the Lost Crusade, there is a scene where Jones and antagonist Donovan think they have found the Holy Grail. The cup that Christ used during the last supper. However, there are many cups on a long table. Most of the cups are beautifully adorned with gold and jewels. The legend as portrayed in the movie was if you drank from the Holy Grail you would have eternal life. Donovan grabbed what he thought looked like a cup representative of a king, drank from it, and instantly aged to death turning into a cloud of dust. The guardian of the Holy Grail, the Grail Knight says, "He chose…poorly." Jones steps up and takes the less attractive cup on the table, stating, "that's the cup of a carpenter." He drinks from the cup and does not turn to dust. The Grail Knight famously says, "You have chosen... wisely!" I use this scene to illustrate the importance of your choice.

Your choices throughout life will determine your life. Everything boils down to a choice. As you think about what I have said regarding forgiveness and reconciliation, I hope you choose wisely. If you do, you will experience a sense of gratitude that will hold your life together. It will be the glue. Strong and sure. It is a glue that cannot be broken. So, let us explore having gratitude.

Chapter Nine

HAVING A SENSE OF GRATITUDE

"Gratitude makes sense of our past, brings peace for today, and creates a vision for tomorrow."

~ Melody Beattie

We all know people who always see life as the glass half-full. They just have a positive attitude and had the ability to maintain that attitude through life's ups and downs. I have always admired those people. However, most of us struggle to maintain a positive attitude throughout all of life's circumstances. I had to remind myself of the blessings I have. Not because I forget, but because life has a way of distracting me. You can imagine how distracted you become at the end of life. There are so many different issues to think about. So, if you are like me, you will need to intentionally prepare for this season of life. As I have said previously, the way you prepare is to practice forgiveness and reconciliation. As you develop the discipline of practicing forgiveness and reconciliation, it will lead you to a sense of gratitude.

This concept of gratitude cannot be understated. Think of it as the glue that holds everything else together. Gratitude becomes especially important at the end of life. In our modern culture death takes many different shapes. Planning for a peaceful death poses different challenges in a private home, a skilled nursing facility, and a hospital. However, most deaths have a few things in common, notably the need for physical comfort, human connection, and pain control. The human connection piece is the focus of this book. Even when physical comfort is available, and pain is being managed if the relationship piece is broken or damaged there will be little peace. Because we tend to die as we have lived, a sense of gratitude or thankfulness allows for the terminally ill person to feel ready to transition from this life.

It is difficult to be grateful for one's life when there are one or more broken relationships. I am referring to significant social relationships, such as family members or close friends. This is why forgiveness and reconciliation are important. When forgiveness and reconciliation have occurred in the relationship, then a sense of thankfulness can be experienced. As I mentioned earlier, Ira Byock, a pioneering hospice doctor coined four simple phrases regarding the management of our relationships. Dr. Byock writes, "Please forgive me," "I forgive you," "Thank you," and "I love you" — carry enormous power to mend and nurture our relationships and inner lives. These four phrases and the sentiments they convey can help us resolve interpersonal difficulties with integrity and grace."[34]

When the terminally ill person is ready to have the "conversation" with family members and friends about their end of life and the others are willing to listen, the stage is set for healing. This is often a difficult conversation as I explained in Chapter One. Using the phrases of Dr. Byock takes humility but can pay huge dividends. The emotion and spiritual sequence to finding peace in the dying process is forgiveness which can lead to reconciliation which can lead to a heart of gratitude. If a person has lived their life with a heart of gratitude, this sequence is made easier. This sequence works both horizontally and vertically, our horizontal relationships with other people and our vertical relationship with God.

What is Gratitude

Gratitude is the expression of appreciation for the good things in one's life. It is the recognition of worth independent of monetary value.

Gratitude is experienced from within and affirms goodness and warmth. This emotion strengthens social relationships and works as a glue to hold them together. Gratitude is a spontaneous feeling and research affirms its value, but it can be intentionally practiced. You can make a conscious effort to count your blessings. Studies have shown that people can deliberately cultivate gratitude. This results in numerous personal benefits.

Why Gratitude is Important

Over the last several decades, there have been numerous studies expressing the many benefits of gratitude. It has been discovered that over time feeling grateful boosts happiness and promotes both physical and psychological health. Gratitude is an emotion, one that lifts your sense of well-being. It is both a temporary feeling and a dispositional trait. As I said earlier, some people are naturally happy. They see the glass half-full. But for the rest of us, we need to intentionally practice gratitude. In other words, you must look for it. When you choose to view life as a precious gift, your inner attention moves away from negative emotions. You harbor less resentment and bitterness. If you are unwilling to live this way, you will be more prone to depression.

People who practice gratitude feel less pain, less stress, sleep better, have a stronger immune system, and enjoy healthier social relationships. As I mentioned, grateful people have less depression and engage in better self-care. Overall, a sense of gratitude can improve your mental and physical health. When you are willing to cultivate gratitude in your life, it generates a climate of positivity. This positivity permeates your being. It reaches inward and extends outward. It changes the way you see the world.

Practicing Gratitude

A sense of gratitude begins when you decide to live each day as if it were your last. I know that sounds like a cliché. However, that does not make it less true. Imagine that you knew today was your last day to be alive. Whatever you do, whatever you say, will be the most important things in your mind and heart. Knowing these would be your last words and actions would change how you lived out this day. There would be people you need to talk with, to tell them you love them. Your significant social relationships would be all consuming. Now imagine, there were several of these relationships that were broken, estranged, and full of bitter feelings. You would do everything possible to fix and heal the brokenness. Why? Because until you do, you will never find peace. It is difficult to experience gratitude when you are not at peace. Gratitude helps you refocus on what you have instead of what you do not have. So how can you cultivate gratitude in your life. Here are some suggestions.

- **Be appreciative of what you have**. I suggest you write down what you are grateful for. Once a week, find a quiet place and reflect. Reflect on your blessings. Write out what you are thankful for in a journal. Think about the entire week and all the things that went well. Here is an example: On Sunday evening, you sit down and write out 3 to 5 things that you really appreciated about the week. As you write, be specific and think about how this blessing made you feel.

  Taking the time to write and keeping a journal is a way to be intentional about staying grateful. It will help you to focus and remember the good things you experienced. This process will speak to your inner self and push out negativity.

- **Maintain a gratitude journal**. If you are practicing being appreciative, you may already be journaling. I would encourage you to write about each day. You could use a journal/calendar. Every day write down what blessings you enjoyed. Then take it a step further and share these moments of blessings with a loved one. The writing and speaking keeps your heart focused on the good rather than the bad.

We all know that life is hard. There is nothing easy about day-to-day living. I am writing during the COVID-19 pandemic, civil unrest in nearly every major city in America, and unemployment at record levels. Moreover, the US economy is in a deep recession. If I did not choose to maintain a sense of gratitude, it would be easy to become negative.

- **Be mental**. I say that with a degree of tongue-in-cheek. Maybe you do not have time to write, but you can think about someone who did something nice for you. I want you to thank them in your mind. Your inner voice, which is in your head, can be positive or negative. Make it positive.

- **Gratitude letter**. Writing a gratitude letter will help make you a happier person and strengthen your relationship with another person. Handwrite this letter. A handwritten letter is becoming a lost art form. Today we text and email. The reason a handwritten letter is powerful is because it takes time and thought. Explain to them your appreciation and enjoyment of the impact they have had on your life. If possible, read your letter to them face to face.

  I encourage you to make this practice a habit. In fact, consider writing and sending one gratitude letter each month. If you do not have time to write a letter, then write a note. A thank you note goes a long way to show our gratitude.

- **Grateful meditation**. This type of meditation focuses on the present moment and what you are grateful for in your life. You may be thankful for the sunshine, or the rain, or whatever. Meditate on how your thankfulness makes you feel.

- **Simple prayer**. I say simple because it does not need to be complicated. Have a conversation with God and thank Him for all the blessings He has given you.

José's Story

I met José while I was on vacation in Mexico. I was walking down the street in Playa del Carmen when I noticed a sign that read, scuba charters. Playa del Carmen is a coastal resort town along the Yucatan Peninsula's Riviera Maya strip of Caribbean shoreline. In the state of Quintana Roo, it is known for its palm-lined beaches and coral reefs. I had read about the extraordinary diving in this area of the Caribbean. I immediately decided to charter a boat and go scuba diving. I have been scuba diving most of my adult life. I have had the privilege to dive in Hawaii, California, Pacific Northwest, and the Bahamas. The next day I came back and met.

As I walked into the small shop, I noticed how simple it was. Certainly not like some of the flashy diving stores I had seen in Hawaii and California. There was no expensive equipment for sale, over-enthusiastic salespeople, or a classroom for teaching the necessary skills to dive safely. It was a space that looked to be 15-by-20 feet, with a small counter at the back. On one wall there were pictures of smiling faces, beautiful looking days on the water, and Capt. José with the biggest smile of all. The other side of the room had a large window that looked out to the ocean. As I walked to the small counter, I noticed a man with his back to me, working on a scuba regulator. I said, "Excuse me, but I am interested in a charter." The man stood, turned, and with the big smile that I noticed in the pictures, thrusted his hand forward and said, "Buenos días, hola cómo estás." I responded, "Sorry, I don't speak Spanish." In his broken English, José said, "Good morning, I'm Capt. José, can I help you?" I was immediately drawn to José. He had a certain look, a charm that I found endearing. When he smiled, his whole face lit up. He was always smiling.

I told him I wanted to charter his boat and go scuba diving. Still smiling, he asked me when I wanted to go? I told him that anytime during the week would be fine. We agreed upon Friday, weather permitting. José informed me the cost of the boat would include two tanks, two dive locations, and his expertise. Laughingly, I said, "Great, I'll see you on Friday." We both said goodbye and I walked out. As I left José's little shop, I was struck by the feeling that I would really enjoy this experience. However, I had no idea how much.

I arrived at the shop Friday morning at 7:30 sharp. As I walked in, I could hear José on the phone and not looking happy. As I reached the counter, José hung up the phone and said, "The other party of six just cancelled." I felt the excitement I had been feeling vanish. I had been on enough charters to know; operators never take out one person. They lose money. I stood there, watching José apparently thinking, when he blurted out, "Amigo, it's a beautiful day, let's go diving." I could not believe it. Taking only me out would cost him money and I could not afford to charter the whole boat. I said, "Capt. José, I can't afford to pay you for the whole boat." José smiled and with a twinkle in his eye said, "No worries, amigo. You pay just for you and we go diving." I immediately felt the excitement return and paid José sixty-five American dollars for a half day. At long last I would have the opportunity to dive in the beautiful blue-green waters off the Yucatan Peninsula. To say I was excited would be an understatement.

I helped José load the boat with the equipment and tanks. It was a beautiful day in paradise. We left the dock and arrived 45 minutes later at our first dive site. José dropped the anchor and within 15 minutes we were in the water. The dive lasted about 50 minutes with a depth of 60 feet. As I suspected, the dive was amazing. Clear water, beautiful aquatic life, and a great dive guide. Capt. José knew the reef well. Once back in the boat, as I rested, José pulled up the anchor and motored to our second spot. After about an hour and some snacks, we were back in the water. The second dive was better than the first. José took me through several short caves and pointed out the beauty of the reef. We were down about 45 minutes at a depth of 30-40 feet. The water temperature was right at 78 degrees, which made both dives perfect.

We were heading back to the dock. As we motored along, José was telling me about how amazing the diving was in this area and how he felt so lucky. During our entire conversation, José was smiling and animated. His excitement for life was apparent. As we shared our stories, we were becoming friends. When we got back to the dock and unloading the equipment, José turned to me and asked, "Señor Terry, would you like to come to my house for dinner?" I was taken back. José's friendship and generosity were as warm as the Caribbean water. I accepted the invitation with the same level of excitement as I had for the day of diving. José gave me directions to his house and said, "Señor Terry, you are welcome anytime. My family and I eat around 6 o'clock." I thanked him and drove to my hotel.

By the time I arrived at my room it was about 3:30, so I decided to relax by the pool. I took a short nap, then got cleaned up and called for a taxi. When I arrived at José's house, I knocked on the door and was greeted by a beautiful young girl. She said, "Hola." At that moment, José appeared in the doorway and said the same thing. I said, "hello," and was invited in. The house was small and simple in its décor. As I met each member of José's family, I was struck by their warmth and friendliness. José's wife, Mary, was elegant and attractive. Her smile was as inviting as José's. They had three beautiful girls, aging from six to twelve. Sofía was six, Isabella was nine, and Luciana was twelve. Once again, I was taken back by the warmth and generosity of this Mexican family. They were treating me like family. Someone they did not know. As I thought about my life in California, I could not remember ever inviting someone to my house that I barely knew. I have had friends come over and bring their friend that I did not know, but never a virtual stranger without someone accompanying them.

As Mary and girls set the table, José and I talked about diving and living in Playa del Carmen. I was becoming fascinated with José's life. He seemed so happy and content. It was odd. At least, odd to me. He obviously did not have much money. By American standards, he was poor, extremely poor. And yet, his positive attitude was infectious. As Mary finished setting the table, she asked me in her broken English, "Señor, I hope you like fish," with a big smile. And I replied, "Yes, ma'am. Very much." Then on José's clue, everyone bowed their heads and he prayed. I could not understand the words until he said, "Amen."

Dinner was simple, baked cod, boiled potatoes, and a papaya vegetable mixture. Dinner was delightful. As we sat around the table eating, the atmosphere in the room was nothing short of joyous. The conversation, the laughter, the smiles, everything communicated a zest for life and happiness.

After dinner, I asked José if we could talk awhile. José answered, "Sì Señor Terry, of course." I told Mary how wonderful dinner had been, then José and I walked outside to the front porch. We sat down and I felt a cool breeze. It was refreshing since the house had no air conditioner. After a few minutes of talking about scuba diving and fishing, I asked José if I could ask him a personal question. He said, "Sì." As I was about to speak, Mary came out with limeade. She smiled and handed me a glass and gave the other glass to Jose´. I commented to José how wonderful Mary was and he agreed. As I took a drink, I looked out and realized how beautiful it was. The ocean was only several hundred yards away. The blue-green color of the Caribbean was intoxicating. I looked back at José and finally said, "José, how do you like your life?" As the words came out of my mouth, I thought how stupid that sounded. But José did not seem to mind. He got a big grin on his face and said, "Señor Terry, I love my life. I have everything I could want. My life is simple but rich. I am grateful for all that God has given me. My family, my work, and my faith." We talked awhile longer. Then I realized it was getting late. I thanked him for his hospitality and said goodbye to Mary and the girls.

As I walked down the street to hail a cab, my heart was full of the kindness I had experienced from this poor Mexican family. I did not know it at the time, but this experience would stay with me the rest of my life. José lived life with a sense of gratitude that defined him. His thankfulness for all that he had, as little as it was, provided a framework for his life. It was this framework that kept him focused on what was important. Faith, family, and enjoyment of life. He was extraordinary.

You Are What You Think

Numerous studies have shown that specific areas of the brain are involved in experiencing and expressing gratitude. Brain scans of individuals given a task that stimulates expressions of gratitude show lasting changes in the prefrontal cortex that strengthen sensitivity to future experiences of gratitude. People who experience the most gratitude and its positive effects tend to exhibit the following:

- Experience a sense of abundance in their lives

- Acknowledge and appreciate the contributions that other people make in their lives

- Acknowledge and appreciate the small pleasures of life

- Realize the importance of experiencing and sharing gratitude with others

These were the characteristics I observed in Jose. He had learned the secret of living well. Whether these characteristics come to you naturally or not, paying attention to life's positives can train your brain to see more of them. The more you experience them, the more you feel grateful. Let me give you example of being intentional about looking for life's positives. I enjoy surfing. When I go to the beach and the weather and surf conditions are good, I feel blessed for receiving the good conditions. It is being intentional with my attitude.

If the conditions were poor, I could still find blessings. A cloudy walk along the beach can be refreshing. The trick is you must be looking for the blessing. You must be intentional. Go through the day paying attention to all the good things that happen to you. Remember them. Make a mental note, or better yet, write them down. Look at the list at day's end and you will be amazed. This will help you cultivate an attitude of gratitude.

Gratitude at the End of Life

Gratitude is important throughout life. However, gratitude is extremely important at the end of life. Having a sense of gratitude when death is near, is the springboard that helps a peaceful transition. According to Shawn Achor, best-selling author on happiness, describes happiness as a "team sport." The strength of our social relationships is the best indicator of how happy and how healthy we are. So, when one or more of these significant social relationships is broken, it impairs your sense of gratitude. The more significant the relationship, the more it impairs your happiness. All the negative emotions that are generated due to these broken significant relationships are exacerbated at the end of life.

Fifteen centuries ago, a young monk named Benedict founded a Christian order and a monastic system to enhance the church. Benedict wrote, *The Rule*, which is a concise literary work that focuses on leadership and managerial practices. Interestingly, within this work Benedict writes, "Keep death at all times before your eyes." He understood the importance of gratitude. He believed that even if you could not be thankful for bad circumstances, you could be thankful for the opportunities that are presented in every moment, even during difficult circumstances. This is a hard truth for most of us to understand and embrace. We find similar language in the Bible. In the writings of the Apostle Paul to the church in Rome, he writes, "And we know that all things work together for good to those who love God, to those who are the called according to His purpose."[35] Is it possible to be thankful at the end of life? I believe it is. Is it possible to experience death and have this horrible event turn into something that is good? Yes, it is possible. Your death can be your final act of love. I will explain this in detail in the coming chapters. Suffice it to say here, that without gratitude your final act will be far less than loving. The only way you arrive at gratitude is through forgiveness and reconciliation.

Here are how these three components work. You need a sense of gratitude for your life to feel ready to transition from this life. When there are broken significant social relationships in your life, you will never feel ready to say goodbye to this life. The only way to restore your broken relationships is to seek forgiveness and hopefully reconciliation. This process always begins with you. Why? Because you do not know if the other person will ever make an attempt at forgiveness. If you refuse to seek forgiveness and the other person never makes an effort, you are stuck. This process will happen throughout your life. But as I have said, at the end of life this process is extremely important. Every emotion at the end of life is heightened. Consequently, whether your emotions are positive or negative, they are exacerbated. The work becomes increasing the positive emotions and decreasing the negative ones. The best way to accomplish this is to make sure your significant social relationships are healthy.

Matthew's Story

A few years ago, I had the privilege to become familiar with Matthew, an 88-year-old Korean war veteran. He had come to my skilled nursing facility for rehabilitation of his left hip. He had fallen and fractured it while water skiing. When I read this in his chart, I must admit I was intrigued. Water skiing at 88 was impressive. I tried water skiing at 38 and nearly died. During my rounds that day I decided to stop in and introduce myself to Matthew.

As I knocked and walked into his room, I noticed a large man lying in bed talking on a cell phone. Matthew was laughing and very animated. He seemed to be enjoying his conversation immensely. I stood there a few seconds; when Matthew looked over and motioned me to come in. I stepped in and waited until he finished his conversation. As he hung-up, he looked over at me and with a big grin said, "Who are you, young man?" I introduced myself and took a seat beside his bed. He reached over and shook my hand, still grinning. I thought to myself, he seems awfully happy to be lying in a skilled nursing facility with a broken hip. Over the next six weeks, I would learn the answer to Matthew's positive attitude. We chatted for about twenty minutes before I left and continued my rounds. I asked Matthew if I could drop by for a visit later in the week. He said, "Sure, anytime." I said goodbye and left.

A few days later I stopped by Matthew's room and he was sitting on the side of the bed. He was attempting to stand up to use the restroom. I quickly walked over and grabbed one of his arms and sat him back on the bed. He looked at me and commented, "I guess it's a bit early to be walking on my own." I said, "Yea, I think it might be." I called for a CNA (certified nursing assistant) to come and give him a hand. As I waited for Matthew's return, I noticed pictures of his family on the dresser. It appeared to be his wife and two children with several grandkids. When Matthew returned, I asked him if these folks were his family and he said they were. As soon as I mentioned his family, that huge grin returned, and I could see the pride in his face. Most of my visit we talked about his family. They were obviously the joy of his life. He told me about his wife of sixty-three years and their two children.   His son was a dentist in southern California and his daughter was a professor. Matthew's six grandkids ranged in ages from 15 to 26. As we talked, I got the sense that Matthew was grateful for his life. I wanted to explore this with him before he left my facility to return home.

The next week I went by Matthew's room, but he was not there. I walked down the hall and looked in the workout room for the rehab patients and there he was. He was walking using a walker across the room. He looked up and saw me standing there. He smiled and said with a sense of pride, "Chaplain Terry, good to see you. I'm finally walking again." I smiled and replied, "Great job Matthew." He had more work to do, so I excused myself and said I would check back with him. It struck me that Matthew was a determined individual. I was hoping to probe deeper into his personal life and better understand his sense of gratefulness.

I did not see Matthew for a week or so. My schedule was busy, and it was difficult to get by his room. When I did stop by, I noticed his bed was made and his pictures were gone. I checked at the nurse's station and was informed he had gone to the hospital several days before. That was not uncommon, so I did not think too much about it. Two weeks passed and I was informed that Matthew had returned but was not there for rehab. He had suffered a blood clot that had damaged his heart. The heart was beyond repair and Matthew was given six weeks to live. Matthew was now in the skilled nursing center waiting to die.

As I was on my way to visit Matthew, I was remembering how happy he had been with his life and his determination to walk again. I could only imagine the Matthew I would soon meet now. I was sure that depression and bitterness would be his companions now. When I reached Matthew's room, I took a breath and turned into the doorway. As I slowly walked in, I noticed the curtain was drawn around his bed, which usually indicates the nursing staff is busy with the patient. I stood there for a moment, then suddenly, I heard the same joyous voice I heard the first time I visited Matthew. I could not believe my ears. At that moment, the nurse pulled the curtain back and Matthew was lying there chatting on his cell phone. Maybe he did not know his prognosis yet. He certainly did not sound depressed or unhappy.

He was laughing and joking with whoever was on the other end of the phone. I was shocked.

I stepped out of the room to give Matthew some privacy. I was talking with a nurse when I heard my name. I walked back into the room and was met with that same huge grin. I said, "Hey Matthew, how are you doing?" Not sure of the response I would get. Matthew quickly replied, "Chaplain Terry, wonderful to see you again. It's been a while." He motioned for me to sit down. For the next several minutes we exchanged small talk. I did not wait to bring up what I had been told about his condition in case he was not aware. Then Matthew blurted out, "Did you hear I am dying?" As I searched for the right words to say, I replied, "Yes, Matthew, I did hear. How are you really doing?"

Matthew started to share with me how he had decided to live his life ever since the war. We spent the next several hours together. I learned more about the importance of gratitude than I had with all the books I had read. Matthew told me he was not particularly a religious person, but during the war he had had a conversation with God. It was during a terrible firefight, and he told God if he survived, he would be grateful the rest of his life. Since Matthew was a man of honor and integrity, he never forgot that promise he made. He promised God that he would be grateful for each remaining day of his life. And he would live each day as his last. Matthew told me he had kept his promise. It was not always easy, but it was a daily decision he made. Then he said, "Just because my life is about over, I'm not about to change my decision. I will be grateful for each day I have, each and every day. Period." Matthew continued sharing with me about what being grateful meant to him. He had worked hard at not living with any type of brokenness. He wanted to live in wholeness. Consequently, every significant social relationship that Matthew had was healthy. There was nothing left undone. He was ready.

Over the next several weeks, I would come by most days and visit Matthew. Often his family were there. I got to know them almost as well as Matthew. Even though there was tremendous grief, there was also a peace. Not only for Matthew, but for his family as well. Marjorie, Matthew's wife, commented to me on several occasions, that he was leaving a wonderful legacy to his family. I said, "Really, what is that Marjorie?" thinking to myself that I already knew. Marjorie looked at me with what I can only describe as peacefulness and said, "Matthew has shown all of us how to die with peace and dignity." As I smiled and gave her a hug, I thought to myself, "Yep, he gave me the same legacy." Matthew's death was truly the final act of love.

It never ceases to amaze me, the extraordinary impact that people have on our lives. Matthew was one of those people. He lived each day to the fullest. Consequently, he died with peace. Never underestimate the power of gratitude. If you are not living with a heart full of gratefulness, figure out why and change it. Now! Tomorrow is not promised to you. If you want your life and death to be a legacy to your family and friends, this is the road you must choose. Choose it today. Do not wait, thinking you have time. If there are broken significant social relationships in your life, make them right. Do whatever it takes. I realize it is not easy; nothing worthwhile ever is. But I promise you it will be worth it. This process will make you feel vulnerable. Keep reading and you will become stronger.

Chapter Ten

VULNERABILITY AND DEATH

*"To share your weakness is to make yourself vulnerable;
to make yourself vulnerable is to show your strength."*

~ Criss Jami

We have all felt vulnerable at one time or another. It is not a pleasurable feeling. In fact, it can be terrifying. This is why we try to avoid it and sometimes avoid it at all cost. The ironic thing, however, is that there is nothing within the human experience that does not bring a certain element of vulnerability. There are social, emotional, financial, and relational insecurities. At the end of life, one or more of these insecurities can be present. Most of us fight our entire lives to avoid being vulnerable. It is not surprising that we fight even harder when our time is coming to an end. In this chapter, I will explain why this season of life is the time to embrace your insecurities and experience freedom.

When you make a smoothie, you put your ingredients into the blender, put the lid in place, and turn it on. Within a few seconds you have a delicious drink. Your vulnerabilities at the end of life are similar. Every insecurity you have experienced and not overcome, comes flooding back into your life; they are all mixed together inside of you and you feel afraid and out of control. The most difficult of these mixed emotions is broken significant social relationships. You know you should reach out, but you are just too afraid. Every relationship comes with a degree of vulnerability. When things are going smoothly, the sense of vulnerability slips into the background of our minds. When things become rocky, that sense of vulnerability comes flooding back. Most of us live within this ebb and flow. As I have demonstrated in this book, repairing broken relationships helps you to live better. It certainly helps you die better.

Is Vulnerability Worth It

Have you ever felt terrified to share with a significant social relationship how much you needed their help or support? Maybe you have avoided bringing up some important issue because you did not want to appear inadequate or uncaring. If you are like most people, there have been times when you pulled back from someone emotionally because you were too overwhelmed with the circumstances. These are natural reactions when you feel vulnerable in a relationship. According to Dr. Geraldine Piorkowski, who authored, *Too Close for Comfort: Explaining the Risk of Intimacy*, "We often become fearful when there is a possibility that our deepest desires could be trampled upon, rejected, or unfulfilled."[36] As uncomfortable as vulnerability feels, it is precisely what allows you to move forward and grow.

Keeping significant relationships at arms-length may feel like you are protecting yourself, but in the long run you are harming yourself. It is impossible to live well when the people most important to you are not allowed into your heart. I want to be clear. Not all your relationships qualify as significant social relationships. You may have friends and colleagues that you think highly of, but who do not rise to the level of significant. Significant social relationships are the most important people in your life. These relationships carry the highest level of emotional investment. When one of these relationships becomes "broken" it is imperative to seek reconciliation. Otherwise, the hurt and anger will fester like a disease and only become worse over time. The first hurdle you face in repairing the significant relationship is vulnerability.

As I have stated, being in a vulnerable emotional state is never easy. It involves tearing down the emotional walls, letting your guard down, and exposing yourself to another human being. Not just any human being, but someone who is important in your life. It is this importance that gives them power over you, which in turn brings feelings of vulnerability. This makes you feel weak and out of control. This is the battle. All these negative feelings. And make no mistake, it is a battle. An emotional and spiritual battle. But here is the bottom line: vulnerability is key in the forgiving and reconciliation process.

Benefits of Being Vulnerable

Culture has a powerful influence over us. So many negative things are reinforced by society. Often our culture teaches you that being dishonest is acceptable behavior-even considered the norm. No one is completely honest. Why not cheat if it brings you an advantage? Being hard and stern will keep your feelings safe. Such misconceptions. Falsehoods such as these and many more, are just that. They are false. Now let us look at a few ways that vulnerability can benefit you.

1. Self-esteem increases

I know this sounds absurd. How can feeling vulnerable impact your self-esteem? Because allowing yourself to feel vulnerable is a show of strength. It takes inner strength and a determination to imagine a better outcome. Digging-in your heels and bragging how tough you are behind the emotional wall you have built accomplishes nothing. Your sense of self-worth goes up because there is power and freedom in forgiveness. Vulnerability helps you to acknowledge that everyone has strengths and weaknesses. When you find the courage to become vulnerable, that opens the pathway for forgiveness and reconciliation.

2. Living in the moment

We all know that living in the moment is important, rather than living in the past. Unfortunately, many of us live all or part of our lives in the past or the future. There was a point in my life when I lived almost exclusively in the future. I was in law school, earnestly desiring to finish and graduate. I did graduate, but also discovered I had missed the journey. I have always regretted that. Today, I work hard to enjoy and appreciate every moment.

Being in the moment and allowing yourself to feel the emotions going on inside you is healthy, both positive and negative. Moreover, communicating your feelings can be liberating. There is a certain freedom that comes with sharing what you are feeling. When you hold your feelings in because you are afraid, it can cause a significant degree of emotional and mental stress. Ongoing chronic stress can cause or exacerbate many serious health problems such as:

- Depression, anxiety, and personality disorders.

- Cardiovascular disease, including heart disease, high blood pressure, abnormal heart rhythms, heart attack, and stroke.

Being in the moment and willing to embrace whatever you are feeling is a positive way to mitigate stressful situations. We all experience stress, but the key is to manage it in a positive way. To avoid difficult situations, while living in the past or future, is counterproductive.

3. A happier you

When you refuse to allow yourself to be vulnerable, you become closed off to your true feelings. When feelings, whether positive or negative, are not given expression, they become bottled up. Positive feelings without expression, lead to frustration. Negative feelings without expression lead to emotional eruption.

Something triggers your negative pent-up feelings and you explode.

Happy people are vulnerable people. To be an authentic person, meaning you desire to live your life being honest, you must be vulnerable. Circumstances arise almost daily in which it may be easier to be less than honest. You do not want to hurt someone's feelings, the truth is more complicated than lying about it, or it is easier to tell the other person what they want to hear. All these outcomes will leave you feeling like a fraud. Truth-telling means to be vulnerable; without it, you will never be happy.

4. Fosters compassion

When someone harms you, the natural reaction is to become defensive. Defensiveness is a self-protective emotional response. Generally, once you become defensive, you then become angry. When you are angry, it is difficult to be objective. Without objectivity, it is difficult to effectively communicate.

A person who understands and practices vulnerability is more likely to take a breath and step back for a moment. When you do this, it gives the other person a chance to be vulnerable. Mutual vulnerability allows both individuals space to be less reactionary. Remember, vulnerability opens the door for humility that can lead to forgiveness and reconciliation. That is the goal: less broken relationships and healthier living.

5. Boosts emotional intimacy

Intimacy can only exist within the walls of vulnerability. However, because of prior hurts, failures, and deep disappointments, allowing yourself to be vulnerable is extremely scary. You are afraid of being hurt again. We have all been there. However, without social intimacy, significant relationships will not thrive. Every important social relationship you have needs to have a corresponding level of emotional intimacy to be healthy.

Practicing vulnerability in your significant social relationships will help keep the communication honest and healthy. I mentioned this in a prior chapter but let me reiterate. You are not a door mat. If the other person has proven themselves to be completely untrustworthy, you must practice *guarded vulnerability*. Someone who continuously emotionally harms you should not have access to hurting you again. You have heard the phrase, "You can lead a horse to water, but you can't make them drink." When the other person refuses to engage in vulnerability towards you, you must move forward with caution. The sequence of humility, vulnerability, forgiveness, reconciliation, and gratitude works best with both parties engaged. However, it is possible to experience these attributes based solely on your desire to achieve them.

Be Patient with Yourself

There is a word I have never been fond of: that word is process. Even though I have improved as I have become older, patience has never been a virtue of mine. Consequently, the meaning of the word process is inherently difficult for me. However, everything I have written about in this book is a "process". Very few good things happen immediately. It takes time. Practicing vulnerability is no exception. Humbling yourself in a healthy way and becoming vulnerable takes practice. Imagine a beautiful brick cathedral or castle. As you stand before it, the architecture is breathtaking. Now imagine how the edifice was constructed-one brick at a time. Building vulnerability into your life is much the same way. As with the beautiful church or castle, your character will shine with beauty.

Remember my personal story in part-one. I believe it accentuates how important it is to allow yourself to be vulnerable. The story I shared with you was an exceedingly difficult time in my life. I am willing to be transparent with one of my many failures, to show you the power of vulnerability.

A New Person

I told you the story in Chapter One so you might better understand where humility and vulnerability can lead you. My greatest moment of vulnerability was a religious experience. Starting a life of faith made me feel extremely vulnerable. Yours may be far different, but the result will be the same. A changed person. The reason that humbling yourself and allowing yourself to be vulnerable is so powerful, is because it leads to forgiveness and reconciliation. Forgiveness and reconciliation can be between you and God, or another person or both. Regardless of where it leads you, it will change your life.

I am a firm believer in second chances. We all make mistakes going through life. Some mistakes are small and insignificant, while others are huge and life changing. Whatever the size of the mistake, I have discovered that allowing myself to be vulnerable is like giving myself a second chance. Giving yourself permission to reach out in hopes of fixing a broken relationship is powerful. The act of reaching out with humility and vulnerability has many benefits previously stated. I encourage you to be brave. I know this is hard. But the potential benefits greatly outweigh the negative feelings you must overcome.

Vulnerability denotes susceptibility to harm and is derived from the Latin *vulnerare*, meaning "to wound." The entire concept of vulnerability is difficult. We are all struggling in our own way. Vulnerability researcher Brene Brown has noted that within the American culture, we are the most in debt, medicated, obese, and stressed people in history.[37] Consequently, it is not surprising that we have many emotional issues trapped inside of us. For all the diversity within our country, we as human beings have many similarities. We desire the same things: to be liked, respected, and feel productive. We want to believe our life matters. That we are significant. Our culture would have us believe that showing only confidence and strength is the key to success. Showing any form of weakness or vulnerability is only a prescription for failure. The truth, however, is just the opposite.

In tough and difficult times, like pandemics and civil unrest, your inner circle can really make a difference in your emotional health. You should never think you can stand alone. You were made for community. So, when someone from your tribe is estranged from you, it is important to find a solution to the problem. The remedy is always forgiveness and reconciliation. The only way to get there is through humility and vulnerability. As scary as it is, become this new person, a person that is courageous and chooses to do what is right. A person who can be vulnerable. To die well, means you need to live well. You cannot live well without being vulnerable.

Chapter Eleven

SPIRITUALITY AND DEATH

"A journey of a thousand miles begins with a single step."

~ Lao Tzu

Your death is really about your journey of life. Every day you wake up in the morning is a day closer to your last day. I do not say this to sound morbid. I say it because it is true and that it should give you encouragement for the new day. Live every day to the fullest. If you are reminded that you have a finite number of days, you are more likely to enjoy and appreciate each of those days. In fact, I would argue that each day of your life holds miracles. Now miracles are interesting. Sometimes they are hugely apparent and other times, they are only a shadow. But when you look closely, you will find *God's fingerprints* on them. In the part-one, I shared with you my story of crisis and redemption. Little did I know, the story would become even more interesting.

I have mentioned on several occasions in this book that forgiveness, reconciliation, and gratitude are part of the human DNA. The reason I believe this is because you are the *Imago Dei* of God. This is Latin for the Image of God. The Image of God is a concept and theological doctrine in Judaism, Christianity, and Sufism of Islam. It asserts that human beings are created in the image and likeness of God. In other words, you have certain attributes as God has. Namely, the capacity for forgiveness, reconciliation, and gratitude (thankfulness). Let us explore what the Bible has to say about these concepts.

A Biblical Perspective

Forgiveness

The Theological Doctrine of Forgiveness is the hallmark of Christian Scriptures. The work of God throughout the ages has been to communicate His forgiveness to humanity. Notwithstanding God's salvific plan, His process of forgiveness is progressive. It begins in Genesis 3:23 when God banishes Adam and Eve from the Garden. Rather than destroying them He allowed them to live. From that point forward there is a progression to God's forgiving grace.

The best example is Joseph's forgiveness of his brothers who had sold him into slavery recorded in Genesis 45:1-15, although this is arguably more a story about reconciliation than it is about genuine repentance and forgiveness. Elsewhere in the Old Testament, the focus is on prayers to God for the forgiveness of wayward individuals or groups, especially through the sacrificial system established with the covenant. Examples include animal atonement offerings in Leviticus 5:14-16, 6:6-7 and Numbers 28. In addition, Job's prayer for pardon in Job 7:21 and Moses' plea for the restoration of Israel in Exodus 32:32. In the prophetic literature, God's forgiving responses are recorded, as in the promise to Jeremiah to restore Israel in Jeremiah 33:8. The Prophet Isaiah asks God to "blot out" and "not remember" Israel's sins in Isaiah 43:25. God's forgiveness stands out as a theme throughout the Old Testament but not necessarily interpersonal forgiveness.

The New Testament continues this concern for forgiveness but with a different focus. The New Testament looks to the "perfect sacrifice" who replaces the old sacrificial system as discussed in Hebrews 10:8-10. Moreover, the New Testament, particularly Jesus' teaching on forgiveness has a more personal feel. At the Last Supper, Jesus declares, "This is my blood of the covenant, which is poured out for many for the forgiveness of sins" (Matthew 26:28).

However, Jesus also offers direct teachings on forgiveness, and it is clear that interpersonal forgiveness is an important concern.

One of the best examples of the interpersonal nature of forgiveness from a New Testament perspective is Jesus' response to Peter in Matthew 18:21-22, "Then Peter came to him and asked, "Lord, how often should I forgive someone who sins against me? Seven times?" "No, not seven times," Jesus replied, "but seventy times seven!" Another famous passage on forgiveness is found in the Lord's Prayer recorded in Matthew 6:12, "Forgive us our trespasses as we forgive those who trespass against us." In Luke's Gospel, Jesus does instruct his followers to "bless those who curse you [and] pray for those who abuse you" (Luke 6:28), which appears to be exactly what he is doing on the cross. And arguably the third most famous verse on forgiveness is Jesus' words from the cross, "Father, forgive them*"* in Luke 23:3. In all four Gospels, Jesus notes the importance of forgiving others to ensure God's forgiveness, and gives more clarification in Luke 17:3 when He says, "If there is repentance, you must forgive."

Throughout the biblical narrative it is evident that God understands the human condition clearly. The brokenness. The depravity. As mentioned above, the human ability to weaponize every aspect of human life. Even religion has been weaponized in history. Maybe that is why God has weaponized forgiveness (in the most positive way). Forgiveness can be either used for defense or offense. It is how we fight against anger and bitterness. It is how we accept love, both God's love and human love. It is our greatest defense against the evil one and our greatest offense to becoming Christ-like.

Reconciliation

Reconciliation in Christian theology is a doctrine that speaks to God's salvation that results from the sacrificial atonement of Christ and the Cross. In other words, biblical reconciliation is the end of the estrangement, caused by original sin, between God and humanity. As with forgiveness, reconciliation represents the very heart of God. The Apostle Paul speaks to this in 2 Corinthians 5:19 when he writes, "For God was in Christ, reconciling the world to himself, no longer counting people's sins against them. And he gave us this wonderful message of reconciliation."[38]

In the above verse, the word "reconciling" is a theological term describing the removal of enmity between humans and God.[39] The Doctrine of Reconciliation paves the way for me to receive God's salvation and by extension share it with others. Reconciliation with God can be the most difficult while at the same time the most uncomplicated. In Matthew's gospel we have these words, "So if you are offering your gift at the altar, and there remember that your brother has something against you, leave your gift there before the altar and go; first be reconciled to your brother and then come and offer your gift."[40] Faith traditions have different ways of approaching reconciliation. From a biblical perspective however, reconciliation begins with God and then can be extended to others.

Based on biblical texts stated above and many others, a strong case can be made regarding the authenticity of human forgiveness without reconciliation. In other words, if I offer the words to someone I have harmed, "I am sorry, will you forgive me?" but refused to be reconciled, there is a clear biblical disconnect. This is different than "forgive and forget." There are harms and injustices that we should never forget. In some cases, our reconciliation is in spirit. I believe this can accomplish the reconciliation that God's requires. Said in a more practical way, I forgive you and feel reconciled before God in this circumstance with you, but I do not feel I can trust you or be in your company.

I had a friend who lost his daughter in a drunk driving accident. My friend was a Christian who was a good man, one that loved the Lord. After months of prayer and counseling he felt ready to forgive the individual who had taken his daughter's life. It was a very difficult journey for my friend. His love for Christ was more powerful than his hatred for the man that took his daughter's life. To keep the story short, my friend finally met with the man and received his apology. My friend extended forgiveness which brought about a spiritual reconciliation. However, my friend was not of a mind to become best friends with this person. My friend finally found peace of heart and mind and gratitude for God's mercy. Interestingly, the Doctrines of Forgiveness and Reconciliation can lead to a heart of gratitude.

Gratitude (Thankfulness)

Having a heart of gratitude or thanksgiving is a biblical imperative. We are told to be thankful numerous times in the writings of the Apostle Paul. In his letter to the Colossians, Paul writes,

> "And let the peace that comes from Christ rule in your hearts. For as members of one body you are called to live in peace. And always be thankful. Let the message about Christ in all its richness, fill your lives. Teach and counsel each other with all the wisdom He gives. Sing psalms and hymns and spiritual songs to God with thankful hearts. And whatever you do or say, do it as a representative of the Lord Jesus, giving thanks through him to God the Father."[41]

We are told three times that the condition of our hearts must be one of thanksgiving. In Chapter Four of the same letter we are told, "Devote yourselves to prayer with an alert mind and a thankful heart."[42] Having a heart full of gratitude toward life allows for the same attitude when facing death.

In the New Testament the verb *eucharisteo* is used thirty-eight times and is translated "to thank or give thanks." When we read this term in the New Testament it is usually referring to thanksgiving toward God. However, in several passages it denotes thanksgiving between human beings.[43] The Apostle Paul uses this word or its variations constantly to express thankfulness of the heart. *Eucharisteo* was used in the blessing before having a meal and we get the word Eucharist for the Lord's Supper.[44] It is a powerful word that shows the importance of being thankful.

I have a friend who each week meets with a group of dynamic seniors living in an assisted-living group home. They chat and drink tea together, and then my friend reads to them. Her assessment of this group is that they choose to focus on what they still have rather than on what they have lost. That attitude makes an immeasurable difference in how they adjust to the losses they frequently face.

After years of ministry and conducting research on this topic, I am convinced that a thankful heart shines a light on how to live and how to die. I am reminded of the saying, "we shall die as we live." Consequently, the words of Apostle Paul in 1 Thessalonians 5:16-18 become even more important, "Always be joyful. Never stop praying. Be thankful in all circumstances, for this is God's will for you who belong to Christ Jesus."[45]

I realize that we experience seasons in our lives that make it difficult to be thankful. Life is difficult at times. Notwithstanding life's ups and downs, as people of faith we should always echo David's Psalm 100, "Shout with joy to the Lord, all the earth! Worship the Lord with gladness, come before him, singing with joy. Acknowledge that the Lord is God! He made us, and we are his. We are his people, the sheep of his pasture. Enter His gates with thanksgiving; go into his courts with praise. Give thanks to Him and praise His name. For the Lord is good. His unfailing love continues, and his faithfulness continues to each generation."[46] Nothing in David's psalm suggests we must be thankful for every circumstance we encounter. It does demand we be grateful for the Lord and his ever-enduring love and faithfulness. God's love and faithfulness transcends this life. Consequently, we can be grateful for him through all life's circumstances-even death.

From the perspective of biblical gratitude, seeing God's fingerprints on every-day events becomes easier. When you are able to see His fingerprints, it is much easier to see His miracles. But remember, you must be looking. Keep your eyes and your heart wide open for his handiwork. You will not be disappointed. When you least expect it, the counsel that is given in Romans 8:28 will be evident, "And we know that in all things God works for the good of those who love him, who have been called according to his purpose."

Forgiveness, Reconciliation, and Gratitude are His Fingerprints

The truth is, that we were created with the purpose that one day we would die. Our bodies are meant to deteriorate over time. Your existence in this life was not intended to last forever. Your soul, on the other hand, was created to last for eternity. As a Christian, I believe that when my life ends here, I will find myself in God's presence. Realizing that one day I will die, drives me into two possible directions which are mutually exclusive.

First Direction:

If you believe that you are mortal and there is no afterlife, you will live your life with anxiety and inner discomfort about your situation. Ernest Becker confirms this in his book, *The Denial of Death.* Becker points out that even though we know we will die; we refuse to acknowledge it. We do everything in our power to deny it. We do not want to think about it and certainly not talk about it. Becker claims that this psychological denial of death is at the heart of the human experience. Consequently, human beings try all sorts of strategies to escape from thinking about their mortality.[47] Whether you accept death or not, we all know it is inevitable. Knowing deep down you are going to die one day you need to find meaning in this life. So, most people attempt to ground themselves in something that feels permanent; this may include science, medical advancements, or relationships.

Living with this belief is mentally, emotionally, and spiritually dangerous. Nothing in this life is permanent. When you put your trust in anything besides God, you will come up short.

Second Direction:

If you believe that you are mortal and there is an afterlife, you will live your life with peace and an expectation for your new life. This is true for reasons already stated. It is a matter of perspective. There will come a time when you must look at dying as your launch date. While I was attending Fuller Theological Seminary working on a master's in divinity, I would take 2-3-day retreats at the Prince of Peace Abbey in Oceanside, California. The Prince of Peace Abbey is a Roman Catholic, Benedictine order of monks, who have built a retreat center on their property and invite anyone who wants to spend quiet time with God. It is a wonderful place for spiritual refreshment and renewal.

During one such retreat, I received a tour of the abbey from the Abbott or head monk. He showed me various places such as the kitchen, dining area, classroom, and offices. The last place he took me was the infirmary. As I looked in, it reminded me of a hospital wing. There were various pieces of medical equipment and six beds lining one wall. As I looked around the room, the Abbott pointed to the beds and with a big smile said, "these are our launching pads." I never forgot that phrase. What a beautiful perspective on death. Death is our launching pad.

In His Grip

The Christian gospel is explicit on life after death. Therefore, as Christians, we should be living our lives knowing we are going to experience a new life. A new resurrected life in Christ. Moreover, we should live this life knowing God created us for something special. I do not know specifically what God has set before you to accomplish during your life. I do know one aspect of what God has called you to do. That is to live well, so you will die well. How you navigate through this life impacts the people around you. How you die, also impacts the people around you. In fact, one of the greatest legacies you can leave is how you die. Passing from this life to the next with peace and dignity will show those who come after you how to do the same.

Remember, how you live impacts how you die. As I have said, forgiveness, reconciliation, and a sense of gratitude are the keys to dying well. As Christians, we should overcome our fear of death. We should celebrate, not death itself, but overcoming the fear. Forgiveness, reconciliation, and gratitude are attributes of the heart of God. Since we are created in the image of God, we too have these characteristics. As human beings, we possess these characteristics for a reason. The reason is this, so that we might live in *God's grip* and extend these attributes to each other as God has extended them to us. God desires to walk with you throughout your life. He wants to do miracles in your life. He will be with you and will never forsake you. He will do this all the way to the end and into the new beginning. He will leave His fingerprints on you all the way into heaven.

Chapter Twelve

QUALITY OF LIFE VS. EXTENDED LIFE

"Life is ten percent what happens to you and ninety percent how you respond to it."

~ Charles Swindoll

People generally want to live as long as possible. I certainly do. But what do you do when the quality of your life is significantly reduced? When you can no longer speak for yourself? When you are lying in ICU and the only thing keeping you alive are machines? What do you do then? These are difficult questions, but extremely relevant. In this chapter, I am going to explore the issues surrounding quality of life verses extended life. It is important to think through these questions and issues before you no longer have the opportunity. Let me say on the outset, I am not advocating physician assisted suicide or euthanasia. I am, however, in favor of following the instructions of the terminally ill patient. I will explain this in more detail later.

If you or loved ones are facing a serious illness, you probably have many questions relating to pain management. You probably have heard the terms "palliative care or hospice care." Maybe you have wondered about the difference. Both are about bringing comfort and relief to the terminally ill. They are, however, different and focus on different aspects of end-of-life care. To make sure you receive the right type of care for your circumstances, you need a good idea of what each type of care provides.

Palliative care got its start as hospice care in 1948. Dame Cecely Saunders, a British physician founded the first formal hospice specifically to care for terminally ill patients. With the birth of palliative and hospice care, there has been a steady growth of understanding about the needs of the terminally ill. In a culture where talking about death and dying is taboo, I am grateful for these two organizations. Hospice and palliative care have substantially given a voice to patients who in the past had no voice about their treatment. Medical procedures were directed entirely by medical professionals. The Hippocratic oath is an oath of ethics that historically every physician took. The oath has been modified over the years, but the basic intent remains, to do no harm and defeat disease. For many years, the Hippocratic oath was interpreted to mean to extend a patient's life at all cost. Death is seen as the enemy; something to be conquered. Fortunately, this has changed over the last 70 years with palliative and hospice care. So, what is the difference between the two?

What is Palliative Care?

Palliative care focuses on easing pain and living with an illness that may become terminal. It helps people live with the symptoms of diseases such as: cancer, kidney disease, or congestive heart failure to name a few. Palliative medicine does not replace other forms of treatment. It is an addition that assists the patient and family members to deal with issues of quality of life. An important focus of palliative care is pain management. If the illness makes it difficult to work, enjoy life, or causes depression, palliative can address that as well. A patient under palliative care generally feels in more control of their life. In cases where the illness is likely to become fatal, palliative care will help with the quality of life and being as active as possible.

What is Hospice Care?

Hospice care focuses on end-of-life care. When a patient has been informed by their doctor that they are not expected to recover from their illness, hospice care is appropriate. It will focus on pain management and preparing the patient and family members for the end of life. People under hospice care generally are expected to have less than 6 months to live. Hospice patients are often at home, with family members or professional caregivers providing the necessary care. However, hospice services are used in skilled nursing facilities and hospitals. Some hospice organizations have their own specialized centers where patients can live out their remaining days.

Hospice care not only includes doctors and nurses, but family members, clergy, counselors, and social workers. It is a holistic model of care that centers on the complete person. This care team addresses pain management, quality of life, and grief counseling. Hospice care is about helping the terminally ill patient to live as comfortably as possible. Managing acute pain is a big part of this.

Summary of Common Areas

Palliative and hospice care are medical specialties aimed at supporting people of all ages with serious, long-term illnesses, including, but not limited to, those listed below:

- cancer

- chronic obstructive pulmonary disease (COPD)

- dementia

- heart failure

- Huntington's disease

- kidney disease

- liver disease

- organ failure

- Parkinson's disease

- stroke

Regardless of the illness, the ultimate goal of both palliative and hospice care is to:

- improve quality of life

- increase overall comfort

- provide emotional support for you and your family

- help you make important decisions about your medical treatment

Neither types of care require you to give up your primary doctor. Both palliative and hospice care will work with your primary doctor to coordinate and manage your care. The table below explains some key differences between palliative and hospice care.

The table below shows the primary differences between palliative and hospice care.

	Palliative Care	Hospice
Who's eligible?	anyone with a serious, long-term illness, regardless of the stage	anyone with a terminal illness whose doctor determines they have less than 6 months to live
What does it involve?	• symptom relief • help making important medical and treatment decisions • emotional, spiritual, and financial support for the patient and their family • assistance in coordinating care	• symptom relief • help making important end-of-life decisions • emotional, spiritual, and financial support for the patient and their family • assistance in coordinating care
Can you still get curative treatments?	yes, if you wish	no, you must stop curative treatments in order to qualify for hospice
Can you still get life-prolonging treatments?	yes, if you wish	no, you must stop life-prolonging treatments in order to qualify for hospice
Who's involved?	a doctor or nurse(s) specializing in palliative care, as	a doctor or nurse(s) specializing in hospice care, as well

	well as other healthcare professionals such as your primary doctor, pharmacists, social workers, and counselors	as other healthcare professionals such as your primary doctor, pharmacists, social workers, clergy, and counselors
Where is it available ?	depending on where you live, home care is sometimes available but is most often offered through a hospital or outpatient clinic	• a hospital • a nursing home • an assisted-living facility • a hospice facility • your own home
How long can you get it for?	depends on your insurance coverage and what treatments you need	as long as you meet the care provider's life expectancy requirements
When can you get it?	as soon as you receive a diagnosis	when an illness is terminal or life-limiting[48]

The End-of-Life Setting

I mentioned in my introduction that 80 percent of people desire to die in their homes. Unfortunately, only 20 percent realize their wishes. When it comes to the issue of quality of life vs. extended life, living out your last weeks and days in your home is better for everyone involved. The setting where end-of-life care is given influences not only the control that the patient and family maintain, but the degree of quality of care the patient receives. In 2004 a study was conducted by Brown Medical School with a focus on quality of care. Their findings indicated that care in the home-setting under hospice care was of higher quality than in institutions, such as hospitals. The study made it clear that "symptom amelioration, physician communication, emotional support, and being treated with respect," was of higher quality than institutional care.[49]

During my tenure at Rosewood Senior Living Community as chaplain, I had numerous opportunities to journey alongside of individuals who were nearing death. Ellen was one of my residents at Rosewood. Her story clearly indicates the evidence stated in the Brown study.

> Ellen, at 86, was a very elegant woman. Her elegance was only matched by her graciousness. Ten years prior, she had been diagnosed with breast cancer. In the last year, Ellen's cancer had returned and spread throughout her chest. It was inoperable and her prognosis was not good. Her doctors had advised that they could attempt surgery but gave her a small window of survival. Returning to a chemotherapy regiment might extend her life for 8-12 months according to her doctors.
>
> Ellen's husband had passed six years earlier and her three children did not live near her. She had no other family. Over the five years I had known Ellen, we became close. She had wonderful stories and she loved to sip tea and share them. I loved to listen. Ellen was an independent resident and had no desire to move into assisted living or the skilled nursing center on campus.
>
> As the days passed, Ellen and I had many conversations about her death. She had decided not to go through chemotherapy again. Ellen wanted to live out her remaining days with the highest quality of life possible. When she told me about her decision, I almost cried. I thought she was giving up. But I was wrong. As we talked about her

decision, I realized just how courageous she was. Ellen had decided to live out her life on her terms. She had no interest in living longer, she wanted to live well, as well as possible under the circumstances.

Without the chemotherapy treatment, her doctors gave Ellen 3-6 months to live. I continued to meet with her daily. She had three requests: she wanted to die in her apartment, she did not want to be in pain, and she wanted her children near her. I told Ellen I would take care of everything.

After several weeks, Ellen's pain was becoming unbearable. With Ellen's approval, I contacted a local hospice organization and they came aboard to help with her care. Hospice professionals have tremendous experience caring for the physical and psychological needs of the dying patient and family members. Hospice is absolutely committed neither to speeding up or slowing down the dying process. They come on the scene when there is no longer hope for recovery. Their primary focus is pain management and making the patient comfortable.

Toward the end, I spent time with Ellen's family and helped guide them through this extraordinary process. I explained that Ellen's lack of interest in food or drink was a normal part of the dying process. Her responsiveness became less and less as the need for morphine increased. My focus turned to Ellen's family. What families require at this point is support and reassurance. They need to know that the pain they are suffering and the sense of guilt they feel for the inability to help their loved one is normal.

Ellen died peacefully in her apartment, surrounded by her family and several friends. Her death was, in my observation, a good death. Ellen had died as she had lived, on her terms. She had peace and felt ready. She had a sense of gratitude right to the end. Ellen, her family, all the hospice professionals and I, believed that her dying was not a failure to overcome her cancer. Rather, it was a success in guiding her through the dying experience.

The space you die in is important. End-of-life care is better when the patient is in simple and comfortable surroundings. Imagine how different Ellen's death would have been in the Hospital. How different would it have been for her family? Ellen's death is also a wonderful testimony for feeling ready to pass. She was grateful for her life even with numerous regrets. She practiced forgiveness and reconciliation throughout her life. I saw firsthand the importance of how you live makes a huge impact on how you die. Ellen had done both well. Consequently, the legacy she left to her children proves the title of this book. Death: the final act of love.

Life is a journey. As with every journey, there are always bumps in the road. We have all experienced getting a curveball thrown at us. In fact, life is made up of many curveballs. How you handle your bumps in the road or curveballs makes all the difference. Facing them is much easier when you can see God's fingerprints on them.

Chapter Thirteen

LEGAL ASPECTS OF DYING WELL END-OF-LIFE PLANNING

"By failing to prepare, you are preparing to fail."

~ Benjamin Franklin

Living well does not happen without intentionality. The same applies to dying well. If you want to experience a peaceful death, you need to plan for it. I know that sounds a bit odd, but it is an important concept. Without planning, all sorts of unforeseen and terrible things can happen, not the least of which is placing a huge burden on your loved ones. To illustrate this point, I have two stories to share with you.

Meet Ruth, she is an eighty-six-old female living in Assisted Living at Rosewood. She was taken to the emergency room by ambulance. Ruth had been found in her room unresponsive and barely breathing. It was later determined that she had a stroke. As Ruth was leaving Rosewood, all her necessary paperwork was given to the EMT's. Her son had been designated as her agent with power of attorney. He was called and met the ambulance at the hospital. Over the past three years, Ruth had experienced several minor strokes and one almost fatal. Ruth had told her son that she did not want to be kept alive if she suffered another debilitating stroke.

After Ruth had been in the ICU for twenty-four-hours, it was determined that she would not regain the ability to communicate. Her son informed the attending physician that she did not want to be hooked up to any machine that would keep her alive. Because of my relationship with Ruth I had driven to the hospital as well. I knew of Ruth's wishes and thought I could help. As it often happens, the attending physician did not agree with the son's request. I introduced myself as the chaplain at Rosewood. I informed the doctor I had heard Ruth share her wishes with her son and that she had shared the same thing with me. Unfortunately, Ruth had never taken the time to complete any advance directives. Consequently, the attending physician still disagreed and refused to take any further responsibility. This was distressing for the family. The whole ordeal had been devastating.

Ruth's primary doctor was notified, and he immediately took responsibility for her care. She was finally moved to a private room and kept comfortable. She was not placed on any lifesaving equipment. Ruth was not eating but could take small amounts of liquid. She was not in pain. Within two days, Ruth was not taking any liquids and was completely unresponsive. Ruth peacefully passed that evening.

I would like you to meet Sam. Sam is an eighty-four-year old male and an independent resident at Rosewood. A week after Ruth had gone to the hospital, Sam went to the emergency room at the same hospital. Sam had suffered a series of small strokes and was unable to communicate. This was completely unexpected by the family. Sam had been highly active for eight-four. He was still driving and taking care of himself. His doctor informed the family that besides the inability to communicate, Sam would be confined to a wheelchair, unable to walk. As I stood with the family in the ICU, the doctor asked if Sam had any advance directives. They responded, no one in the family ever wanted to talk about death. Certainly not death of a loved one. Consequently, there were no advance directives.

While Sam was in the ICU he was placed on a respirator. He was unable to breathe on his own. In addition, Sam had to be place on artificial nutrition and hydration. He opened his eyes from time to time but did not seem to recognize anyone. Sam spent a week in the ICU before he was stabilized. Shortly thereafter, he was transported back to Rosewood's skilled nursing center. Sam lived another forty-eight days in the same condition he arrived with. During this time, I visited Sam frequently and talked with family members. I knew the last month and half of Sam's life had been excruciating for the family. They never wanted to keep Sam alive this way. Apparently, Sam had told his family that he never wanted to end up like he did. Everyone was suffering from guilt and the loss of a loved one.

During the last week of Sam's life, I asked his daughter why they had never drafted any advance directives. She replied, "No one in my family every wanted to talk about death and dying." She continued telling me about how her father had brought it up once over dinner, but no one would engage with him. Our conversation broke my heart. So much grief and sorrow could have been avoided with planning. I never saw Sam's family again, but I never forgot the hard lessons they had all learned. Planning for one's death is an important aspect of dying well.

Medical technology has advanced significantly over the last century. Health professionals have the ability to sustain life far beyond what was previously anticipated. This has caused numerous issues, not the least of which is the additional financial burden on patients, family members, and health institutions. Besides the practical financial issues, there are ethical questions as well. There are individuals who feel that everything should be done to keep a patient alive no matter what the possible expense might be. The other side of that coin speaks to the patient rights. There are those who feel that patients should have the right to determine whether to be kept alive by advanced medical procedures. This debate centers on whether these types of medical procedures are in the best interest of the patient.

Author Daniel Callahan explains it this way: "Constant clinical innovation has made it increasingly hard to know when someone is dying; the line between living and dying has become steadily more obscure."[50] Many questions for patients, family members, physicians, and health professionals involves not only medical issues, but theological and ethical issues as well. Margaret Mohrmann, a theologian and medical doctor, writes, "our adoration of machine and high-tech procedures is a superficial issue and its elimination…would still leave intact the deeper idolatry that supports it, the idolatry of health and the idolatry of life.[51] Dr Mohrmann also states that our health is important and good "only insofar as it enables us to be the joyful, whole person God has created us to be and to perform the service to our neighbors that God calls us to perform…Health is to be sought in and for God, not instead of God.[52]

Legal Precedents

In law school I took a course that focused on end-of-life issues. We thoroughly studied several landmark cases that have significantly changed the debate. The first case we studied was not actually about end of life. It was more about the right of a person to refuse a physical exam. The Supreme Court wrote in 1891:

> No right is held more sacred, or is more carefully guarded by the common law, than the right of every individual to the possession and control of his own person, free from all restraint or interference of others, unless by clear and unquestionable authority of law.[53]

This case involved a woman who refused a surgical procedure to ascertain her injuries. The Supreme Court upheld her right to refuse such examination.

Another important early case was decided by the US Supreme Court in 1914. In *Schloendoff v. Society of New York Hospital*, Justice Benjamin Cardozo wrote, "every human being of adult years of sound mind has a right to determine what shall be done with his own body."[54] This ruling became an important precedent known as "informed consent." It was the ruling that established that an adult has a right to decide what happens to their own body. Moreover, it made clear that an adult is entitled to determine what medical care and procedures they will receive. Their choices must be respected by health professionals. The concept of a medical directive was conceived from this ruling. In addition, this ruling established that a person who is competent and in reasonable health, can make decisions about what medical care they desire if they become incompetent and/or are unable to communicate with medical-care providers.[55]

The legal right of a competent patient to refuse life-sustaining medical care was established in two landmark cases.[56] The first was *Bartling v. Supreme Court* (1984), where the California Court of Appeals held that a patient could be removed from a mechanical ventilator at his request and over the objection of his physician and the hospital. The second case was *Bouvia v. Supreme* Court (1986), once again before the California Court of Appeals, which found that a conscious and competent hospitalized patient who was in severe and acute pain could refuse nutrition and hydration with the understanding that it would end their life.

Several other landmark cases help to set the precedent that competent patients have rights that cannot be ignored. The Quinlan and Cruzan decisions along with the Terri Schiavo case helped to change and reshape the way people consider advanced life-sustaining procedures. For the first time, machinery that might keep someone alive for an indeterminate period of time, particularly if significant improvement is unlikely, can be terminated. These cases allowed for the consideration of "quality of life" to be a determining factor.

Karen Ann Quinlan's family appealed her case to the US Supreme Court in 1976. Karen was 21 years old when she stopped breathing after ingesting alcohol and tranquilizers at a party. Karen had persisted in a vegetative state for several years and her parents wanted her removed from life support. She was receiving artificial nutrition and hydration through feeding tubes and breathing was supported by a mechanical respirator. The decision from the Supreme Court allowed for the respirator to be removed. Karen continued in the vegetative state for another ten years until she died from pneumonia. There was never a ruling on the feeding tubes.

Nancy Beth Cruzin, sustained life-threatening injuries in a vehicle accident in the 1980s. She was left in a persistent vegetative state with no higher-brain function and was kept alive through feeding tubes and twenty-four-hour medical care. After several years, her parents filed a case against the health care facility for refusing to remove Nancy from her feeding tubes. The case made it to the US Supreme Court, which ruled that the wishes expressed by Nancy regarding her medical treatment must be respected. The case was sent back to the Missouri Supreme Court to determine, whether or not Nancy's parents had "clear and convincing evidence" of Nancy's wishes regarding being kept alive artificially. The court was persuaded, and the feeding tubes were removed. Nancy died shortly thereafter in December 1990.

In February 1990, Terri Schiavo suffered a cardiac arrest and severe loss of oxygen to her brain. She was 41 years of age. Shortly after, Terri was taken to a nursing home where she was in a persistent vegetative state. Terri's parents refused to accept the diagnosis of "brain dead" and believed that she responded to their voices and made purposeful movements. Terri's husband had been told by Terri prior to her condition that she did not want to be kept alive if ever she was in such a vegetative state. Her husband filed a petitioned to have the feeding tube that provided all of Terri's nutrients to be disconnected. Her parents legally fought against the removal.

Mr. Schiavo was in and out of court many times beginning in 2001. In 2005, the US Supreme Court eventually refused to grant a stay and the feeding tube was removed. Terri died on March 31, 2005. An autopsy revealed that her brain damage was severe. The damage left her unable to think, feel, see, or interact in any way with her surroundings. This case accentuates the importance of advance directives. The pain and suffering that family members endure when it is not clear what the patient wants at end of life is extensive.

What is Advance Care Planning

It should be noted that each state determines what is legally acceptable to act as an advance directive. Each state is different. To assure that you are acquainted with current legal requirements in your state, check online resources to educate yourself or contact a lawyer. I will provide an overview of what is generally acceptable in most states. As discussed, today there are treatments that can keep patients alive for longer than ever before. Your medical choices need to be made now. Are there treatments you do not want? Where do you hope to spend your last days? Your loved ones must know what to do if you are unable to speak for yourself.

Being extremely sick or injured comes with many challenges. You may feel confused and unsure about the future. You can prepare for these uncertain times with advance care planning. As difficult as it is, deciding, discussing, and documenting healthcare wishes is extremely important as the case above points out. Making healthcare decisions for yourself before you get ill or injured is called "advance care planning." Advance care planning is important for sick and healthy people of all ages. Making choices now can help avoid confusion and frustration in the future. There are 3 steps to advance care planning:

Step 1 - DECIDE

Later in this chapter I will guide you through this first step. Suffice it to say here, intentionally deciding to think about questions that will help you confirm your values, is an important first step. These questions will help you decide on what type of care you want if you become ill.

Step 2 - DISCUSS

Once you have thought about your values and wishes, talk about them often, particularly with your loved ones. Also talk with everyone who might be involved with your care. This may be the most important step in the advance care planning. Talking clearly about your wishes can help make it more likely your wishes will be followed.

Step 3 – DOCUMENT

Once you have talked about your wishes, put them in writing. You can write your wishes in a form called advance directive. There are also forms you can ask your physician to fill out. Please note, it is imperative than you put your wishes in writing. Several of the cases stated above illustrate the disastrous results when a patient's wishes are not written down.

What is an Advance Directive?

Advance directives are forms that record your healthcare wishes in case you cannot speak for yourself. Standard care in a medical emergency may use life-sustaining treatments such as CPR, feeding tubes and ventilators (breathing machines) to keep you alive. These treatments help many people. But they may be harmful in some cases. An advance directive can help give you control over the care you desire.

Please note that advance directives might not be honored if 911 is called. Emergency medical services (EMS) must attempt to save your life *unless* you have a DNR or POLST form which I will discuss later. The DNR or POLST must be visible to the emergency personnel.

What You Must Know:

• Advance directive (AD) takes effect when you cannot speak for yourself. You can make choices if you can think clearly and act on your own. Some states let you apply AD's right away.

• You may not need to fill out an AD if -- no matter what happens -- you want all life-sustaining treatments. However, most healthcare experts say it is always best to complete an AD, so your wishes are clear.

• Your family and care team may need to make decisions for you if you do not have an AD. A court may decide what is best for you if your family and care team disagree about your care.

• You can cancel or change your AD's any time. Let anyone who might be involved with your care know if there are changes. To cancel an AD, you can destroy the form or fill out a new form. You can also write, sign, and date a letter to your care team to cancel; or ask your healthcare agent to write the letter for you.

• You do not need a doctor to sign your AD. You complete an AD on your own, though some people choose to work with their estate lawyer or care team.

• The sections you complete still apply if you skip a section.

• Your state might void your AD if you are pregnant. Some states have laws that protect the fetus in certain cases. Some states let you choose what you would want if you are pregnant.

• If your child is 18 (in some states, 19) years or older and they want you to be involved in their care, they should complete an AD. If not, you might need court approval to speak for them.

Note: Other names for advance directives: living will and durable power of attorney for health care, medical directive, healthcare directive, declaration, healthcare proxy.

Parts of an Advance Directive

Each state's forms vary based on its laws. Most AD's have 4 main parts. Your state may not have all of them, or the sections may be combined. Some states include other sections or instructions. You can get the forms free of charge at www.caringinfo.org/stateADdownload.

Durable Power of Attorney for Health Care

This legal form names a person as your healthcare agent. Your healthcare agent will make medical decisions for you if you cannot speak for yourself. They must be 18 (or 19) years or older. Your state may have other rules about who can be your agent.

Naming an agent does not take away your rights to make your own choices. You do not have to name an agent. Your next of kin will be asked to speak for you if you do not name someone.

Your agent should be:

- Someone who knows you well, lives close by, and knows your values
- Someone who will carry out your wishes, whether or not they agree with them
- Someone who is not afraid to speak up for you, whom you trust, and who is stable
- One person, instead of a group, to avoid arguments

Your agent may need to:

- See your medical records, keep track of your changing health, talk to the care team, ask questions, and make sure your AD is followed
- Decide who will care for you and where care will be given
- Say yes or no to treatments/tests and make choices on things you did not talk about (with the care team's guidance)
- Work with the person in charge of your money (if that is someone other than your agent) to set up payment for care
- Make choices for your body after death (such as organ donation, etc.)

Before naming an agent, discuss your wishes and values regarding end of life. Some states require the agent to accept by signing the AD. You may also want to name a backup agent.

Health Care Agent Form

Your birth date: _____/_____/_____

I, ____, residing at
Principle: Print your name

____
Street   *City/Town*   *State/ZIP*

appoint as my health-care agent:

*Name of person you choose as agent:*________________________

of____
Street   *City/Town*   *State/ZIP*   *Telephone*

Optional: If my agent is unwilling/unable to serve, then I appoint as my alternate agent:

*Name of person you choose as agent:*________________________

of____
Street   *City/Town*   *State/ZIP*   *Telephone*

My agent shall have the authority to make all health-care decisions for me, including decisions about life-sustaining treatment, subject to any limitations I state below, if I am unable to make health-care decisions myself. My agent's authority becomes effective if my attending physician determines in writing that I lack the capacity to make or to communicate health-care decisions. My agent is then to have same authority to make health-care decisions as I would if I had the capacity to make them, EXCEPT (list here the limitations, if any, you wish to place on your agent's authority; if none, enter "none"):

I direct my agent to make health-care decisions based on my agent's assessment of my personal wishes. If my personal wishes are unknown, my agent is to make health-care decisions based on my agent's assessment of my best interests. Photocopies of this Health

Care Proxy shall have the same force and effect as the original and may be given to other health-care providers.

An optional statement is attached (*check one*): _____ yes   _____ no

[You may attach to this document, as a guide to your agent, a statement of particular wishes you want followed by your agent. This is not required, and, in its absence, your agent will use his/her discretion to do what he/she feels you would want done, as a result of discussions you have had with your agent.]

Signed:

____

Complete only if principal is unable to sign: I have signed the principal's name above at his/her direction in the presence of the principal and two witnesses.

____
Name

____
Street   *City/Town*   *State/ZIP*

Witness statement: We, the undersigned, each witnessed the signing of this Health Care Proxy by the principal or the direction of the principal and state that the principal appears to be at least eighteen years of age, of sound mind, and under no constraint or undue influence. Neither of us is named as the health-care agent or alternate agent in this document. In our presence this

______________________ day of ________________________ , ______________________
                                   Month   *Year*

Witness #1 ____
        Signature

____
Print name

____
Street   *City/Town*   *State/ZIP*

Witness #2 ____
        Signature

____
Print name

____
Street   *City/Town*   *State/ZIP*

Statement of Health-Care Agent and Alternate Agent
(*Optional*)

Health-Care Agent: I have been named by the principal as the principal's health-care agent by this Health Care Proxy. I have read this document carefully, and I have personally discussed with the principal his/her health care wishes at a time of possible incapacity. I know the principal and accept this appointment freely. I am not an operator, administrator or employee of a hospital, clinic, nursing home, rest home, soldiers' home, or other health facility where the principal is presently a patient or resident or has applied for admissions. Or if I am a person so described, I am also related to the principal by blood, marriage, or adoption. If called upon and to the best of my ability, I will try to carry out the principal's wishes.

Signature of Health-Care Agent:

____

Alternate Agent: I have been named by the principal as the principal's health-care agent by this Health Care Proxy. I have read this document carefully, and I have personally discussed with the principal his/her health care wishes at a time of possible incapacity. I know the principal and accept this appointment freely. I am not an operator, administrator or employee of a hospital, clinic, nursing home, rest home, soldiers' home, or other health facility where the principal is presently a patient or resident or has applied for admissions. Or if I am a person so described, I am also related to the principal by blood, marriage, or adoption. If called upon and to the best of my ability, I will try to carry out the principal's wishes.

Signature of Alternate Agent:

____

Optional Attachment to Health Care Proxy Form

[You may attach to your medical proxy statement of optional instructions to your agent – or a page of similar language and instructions of your own choosing.]

Statement of my particular wishes: I do not want my life to be prolonged nor do I want life-sustaining treatment to be provided or continued if my agent believes the burdens of the treatment outweigh the expected benefits. My particular wishes are that if I have such an illness, injury or condition, or if I am so mentally impaired that there is no significant quality of life to my existence, and if there is no reasonable expectation of recovery to a state of good quality of life, or if I am permanently unconscious (in a "persistent vegetative state"), that nothing be done to prolong my life, including resuscitative measures (in the event of hypotension, stopping breathing, or cardiac arrest), the administration of intravenous and/or nasogastric fluids and nutrition, the use of respirators or other mechanical devices to sustain life, and the use of antibiotics for pneumonia or other infections (this list is not all-inclusive). With respect to nutrition and hydration provided by means of a nasogastric tube or tube in the stomach, intestines, or veins, I wish to make clear that I intend to include these procedures among the "life-sustaining procedures" that may be withheld or withdrawn under the conditions above.

If I am in the circumstances described above and am in a dying state, I would prefer treatment at home or in a nursing home, with comfort care being the only objective, as opposed to transfer to a hospital, unless the latter were needed for the accomplishment of comfort care, and I request that adequate medication be given to control pain and/or agitation, even if such medication were to result in depressing respiration or hastening the end of life. I want my agent to consider the relief of suffering, the expense involved, and the quality as well as the extension of my life in making the decision concerning life-sustaining treatment.

Note: Other names for a healthcare agent: surrogate, proxy, executor, representative, healthcare power of attorney (POA), attorney in fact, advocate.

Living Will

This form lets you choose life-sustaining treatments (CPR, feeding tubes, ventilators) if you are dying or are permanently unconscious (such as a coma). Each state's living will is different. Some let you choose options based on your condition. Some have you agree or disagree with a list of statements. Many have statements about comfort care and pain relief. Most have space where you can write other wishes.

A living will simply expresses your wishes for end-of-life care. It is not a legally binding document, but usually is honored. It can be an important and useful instrument in conjunction with a medical proxy statement. A living will may state anything you wish regarding your preferences. I have included a sample here. You may alter it in any way you wish. It does not require an attorney – only two witnesses.

Living Will Declaration

To my family, doctors, and all those concerned with my care:

I, _______________________________________, being of sound mind, make this statement as a directive to be followed if for any reason I become unable to participate in decisions regarding my medical care.

I direct that life-sustaining procedures should be withheld or withdrawn if I have an illness, disease, or injury, or experience extreme mental deterioration, such that there is no reasonable expectation of recovering or regaining a meaningful quality of life. Life-sustaining procedures that may be withheld or withdrawn include, but are not limited to: surgery, antibiotics, cardiopulmonary resuscitation, respiratory support, and artificially administered feeding and fluids.

I further direct that treatment be limited to comfort measures only. I wish medication for pain and other distress to be used liberally in doses sufficient to relieve my symptoms, even if such medication were to shorten my life.

Other Personal Instructions

These directions express my legal right to refuse treatment. Therefore, I expect my family, doctors, and all those concerned with my care to regard themselves as morally bound to act in accord with my wishes, and, in so doing, to be free from any liability for having followed my directions.

Signed:____Date:__________

Witnessed: ____

Witnessed: ____

Note: Other names for a living will: declaration, healthcare instructions, healthcare choices, treatment preferences.

Organ donation

This form lets you say yes or no to organ donation at death. Your family will be asked about organ donation if you die in a hospital. They will need to decide right away. Most states add this as an extra form after the AD. Some combine it with the living will.

Many states let you choose options for donation. Others give your agent the power to choose options for you. A few states also ask about autopsy and burial wishes. There is no cost to you or your family if you donate. Go to www.organdonor.org for more information.

Signature and witness

This is where you sign and date the form to confirm you understand the choices you have made. Most states also need 2 witnesses to sign. This makes the AD a legal document. Many states allow a notary to sign instead of 2 witnesses. A few states *require* a notary to sign.

Note: Other names for this section: execution, affidavit.

Other Advance Care Planning Forms

Other advance care planning forms include DNR and POLST. These are medical orders if you are seriously ill or near the end of life. These forms must be signed by you or your agent and a physician. Some states let a nurse practitioner or physician assistant sign them. They are added to your medical record so healthcare staff – including EMS – know our wishes. It is a good idea to complete these forms if you need them, but it is not required.

DNR (Do Not Attempt Resuscitation) Order

This form tells healthcare staff not to use CPR (cardiopulmonary resuscitation) if your heart/breathing stop. There may come a time when you and your care team decide the risks of CPR are too great. Ask your care team about a DNR order at that time. Talk to your care team about the pros and cons of CPR if you are 65 years old or over, are frail, depend on another for care, have more than one serious health issue, or have an end-stage illness.

If you get a DNR order, let everyone who may be involved in your care know you have one. Talk to your healthcare agent, family, care team, and others. Post copies of your DNR on your fridge, inside your front door, and wherever they can be easily seen. Consider buying a medical ID card or jewelry.

Note: Other names for a DNR order: DNAR, DNRO, AND (Allow Natural Death), No Code, No CPR.

Pre-Hospital Do Not Resuscitate (DNR) Form

I, _________________________________, request limited emergency care as herein described.

I understand DNR means that if my heart stops beating or if I stop breathing, no medical procedure to restart breathing or heart functioning will be instituted.

I understand this decision will not prevent me from obtaining other emergency medical care by prehospital emergency medical care personnel and/or medical care directed by a physician prior to my death.

I understand that I may revoke this directive at any time by destroying this form and removing any "DNR" medallions.

I give permission for the information to be given to the prehospital emergency care personnel, doctors, nurses or other health personnel as necessary to implement this directive.

I hereby agree to the "Do Not Resuscitate" (DNR) order.

Signature:____Date:__________

____

Surrogate's Relationship to Patient

By signing this form, the surrogate acknowledges that his request to forgo resuscitative measures is consistent with the known desires of, and with the best interest of, the individual who is the subject of this form.

I affirm that this patient/surrogate is making an informed decision and that this directive is the expressed wish of the patient/surrogate. A copy of this form is in the patient's permanent medical record.

In the event of cardiac or respiratory arrest, no chest compressions, assisted ventilations, intubation, defibrillation, or cardiotonic medications are to be initiated.

____

Physician Signature   Date

____

Print Name   Telephone

DNR Form for the State of California

CMA PUBLICATIONS 1(800) 882-1262 www.cmanet.org

**EMERGENCY MEDICAL SERVICES
PREHOSPITAL DO NOT RESUSCITATE (DNR) FORM**

I, ____ , request limited emergency care as herein described.
(print patient's name)

I understand DNR means that if my heart stops beating or if I stop breathing, no medical procedure to restart breathing or heart functioning will be instituted.

I understand this decision will not prevent me from obtaining other emergency medical care by prehospital emergency medical care personnel and/or medical care directed by a physician prior to my death.

I understand that I may revoke this directive at any time by destroying this form and removing any "DNR" medallions.

I give permission for this information to be given to the prehospital emergency care personnel, doctors, nurses or other health personnel as necessary to implement this directive.

I hereby agree to the "Do Not Resuscitate" (DNR) order.

____   _______________________
Patient/Surrogate Signature   Date

____
Surrogate's Relationship to Patient

By signing this form, the surrogate acknowledges that this request to forgo resuscitative measures is consistent with the known desires of, and with the best interest of, the individual who is the subject of this form.

I affirm that this patient/surrogate is making an informed decision and that this directive is the expressed wish of the patient/surrogate. A copy of this form is in the patient's permanent medical record.

In the event of cardiac or respiratory arrest, no chest compressions, assisted ventilations, intubation, defibrillation, or cardiotonic medications are to be initiated.

____   _______________________
Physician Signature   Date

____   _______________________
Print Name   Telephone

THIS FORM WILL NOT BE ACCEPTED IF IT HAS BEEN AMENDED OR ALTERED IN ANY WAY

PREHOSPITAL DNR REQUEST FORM

POLST (Physician Orders for Life-Sustaining Treatment)

This form tells healthcare staff which treatments you want (or do not want) when you are seriously ill. POLST forms do not replace AD – these forms work together. An AD is filled out ahead of time in case you get sick. A POLST form is filled out only if you are seriously ill. Not everyone with an AD needs POLST. But if you have POLST, it is wise to also have an AD. If you have both, be sure the documents agree with each other. Ask your care team for help, if needed.

Each state has their own version of POLST. Most forms include choices for DNR, level of treatment, and feeding tubes. Some states include other options. Go to www.POLST.org for more information. See an example of a POLST form below.

Note: Other names for POLST: MOLST or COLST (Medical/Clinician Orders for Life-Sustaining Treatment), or MOST or POST (Medical/Physician Orders for Scope of Treatment), TOPP or TPOPP (Transportable Physician Orders for Patient Preference), SAPO (State Authorized Portable Orders).

HIPAA PERMITS DISCLOSURE OF POLST TO OTHER HEALTH CARE PROVIDERS AS NECESSARY

Physician Orders for Life-Sustaining Treatment (POLST)

EMSA #111 B
(Effective 4/1/2017)*

First follow these orders, then contact **Physician/NP/PA.** A copy of the signed POLST form is a legally valid physician order. Any section not completed implies full treatment for that section. **POLST complements an Advance Directive and is not intended to replace that document.**

Patient Last Name:	Date Form Prepared:
Patient First Name:	Patient Date of Birth:
Patient Middle Name:	Medical Record #: *(optional)*

A
Check One

CARDIOPULMONARY RESUSCITATION (CPR): *If patient has no pulse and is not breathing.*
If patient is NOT in cardiopulmonary arrest, follow orders in Sections B and C.

☐ **Attempt Resuscitation/CPR** (Selecting CPR in Section A **requires** selecting Full Treatment in Section B)

☐ **Do Not Attempt Resuscitation/DNR** (Allow Natural Death)

B
Check One

MEDICAL INTERVENTIONS: *If patient is found with a pulse and/or is breathing.*

☐ **Full Treatment** – primary goal of prolonging life by all medically effective means.
In addition to treatment described in Selective Treatment and Comfort-Focused Treatment, use intubation, advanced airway interventions, mechanical ventilation, and cardioversion as indicated.

    ☐ *Trial Period of Full Treatment.*

☐ **Selective Treatment** – goal of treating medical conditions while avoiding burdensome measures.
In addition to treatment described in Comfort-Focused Treatment, use medical treatment, IV antibiotics, and IV fluids as indicated. Do not intubate. May use non-invasive positive airway pressure. Generally avoid intensive care.

    ☐ *Request transfer to hospital only if comfort needs cannot be met in current location.*

☐ **Comfort-Focused Treatment** – primary goal of maximizing comfort.
Relieve pain and suffering with medication by any route as needed; use oxygen, suctioning, and manual treatment of airway obstruction. Do not use treatments listed in Full and Selective Treatment unless consistent with comfort goal. *Request transfer to hospital only if comfort needs cannot be met in current location.*

Additional Orders: ____

C
Check One

ARTIFICIALLY ADMINISTERED NUTRITION: *Offer food by mouth if feasible and desired.*

☐ Long-term artificial nutrition, including feeding tubes.   Additional Orders: ____________________

☐ Trial period of artificial nutrition, including feeding tubes. _______________________________

☐ No artificial means of nutrition, including feeding tubes. _______________________________

D

INFORMATION AND SIGNATURES:

Discussed with: ☐ Patient (Patient Has Capacity)   ☐ Legally Recognized Decisionmaker

☐ Advance Directive dated _______, available and reviewed →
☐ Advance Directive not available
☐ No Advance Directive

Health Care Agent if named in Advance Directive:
Name: ___________________________________
Phone: __________________________________

Signature of Physician / Nurse Practitioner / Physician Assistant (Physician/NP/PA)
My signature below indicates to the best of my knowledge that these orders are consistent with the patient's medical condition and preferences.

Print Physician/NP/PA Name:	Physician/NP/PA Phone #:	Physician/PA License #, NP Cert. #:
Physician/NP/PA Signature: *(required)*		Date:

Signature of Patient or Legally Recognized Decisionmaker
I am aware that this form is voluntary. By signing this form, the legally recognized decisionmaker acknowledges that this request regarding resuscitative measures is consistent with the known desires of, and with the best interest of, the individual who is the subject of the form.

Print Name:	Relationship: *(write self if patient)*
Signature: *(required)* Date:	Your POLST may be added to a secure electronic registry to be accessible by health providers, as permitted by HIPAA.
Mailing Address (street/city/state/zip): Phone Number:	

SEND FORM WITH PATIENT WHENEVER TRANSFERRED OR DISCHARGED

*Form versions with effective dates of 1/1/2009, 4/1/2011, 10/1/2014 or 01/01/2016 are also valid

HIPAA PERMITS DISCLOSURE OF POLST TO OTHER HEALTH CARE PROVIDERS AS NECESSARY

Patient Information

Name (last, first, middle):	Date of Birth:	Gender: M F

NP/PA's Supervising Physician	**Preparer Name** (if other than signing Physician/NP/PA)	
Name:	Name/Title:	Phone #:

Additional Contact　　　　☐ None

Name:	Relationship to Patient:	Phone #:

Directions for Health Care Provider

Completing POLST

- **Completing a POLST form is voluntary.** California law requires that a POLST form be followed by healthcare providers, and provides immunity to those who comply in good faith. In the hospital setting, a patient will be assessed by a physician, or a nurse practitioner (NP) or a physician assistant (PA) acting under the supervision of the physician, who will issue appropriate orders that are consistent with the patient's preferences.
- **POLST does not replace the Advance Directive.** When available, review the Advance Directive and POLST form to ensure consistency, and update forms appropriately to resolve any conflicts.
- POLST must be completed by a health care provider based on patient preferences and medical indications.
- A legally recognized decisionmaker may include a court-appointed conservator or guardian, agent designated in an Advance Directive, orally designated surrogate, spouse, registered domestic partner, parent of a minor, closest available relative, or person whom the patient's physician/NP/PA believes best knows what is in the patient's best interest and will make decisions in accordance with the patient's expressed wishes and values to the extent known.
- A legally recognized decisionmaker may execute the POLST form only if the patient lacks capacity or has designated that the decisionmaker's authority is effective immediately.
- To be valid a POLST form must be signed by (1) a physician, or by a nurse practitioner or a physician assistant acting under the supervision of a physician and within the scope of practice authorized by law and (2) the patient or decisionmaker. Verbal orders are acceptable with follow-up signature by physician/NP/PA in accordance with facility/community policy.
- If a translated form is used with patient or decisionmaker, attach it to the signed English POLST form.
- Use of original form is strongly encouraged. Photocopies and FAXes of signed POLST forms are legal and valid. A copy should be retained in patient's medical record, on Ultra Pink paper when possible.

Using POLST

- Any incomplete section of POLST implies full treatment for that section.

Section A:

- If found pulseless and not breathing, no defibrillator (including automated external defibrillators) or chest compressions should be used on a patient who has chosen "Do Not Attempt Resuscitation."

Section B:

- When comfort cannot be achieved in the current setting, the patient, including someone with "Comfort-Focused Treatment," should be transferred to a setting able to provide comfort (e.g., treatment of a hip fracture).
- Non-invasive positive airway pressure includes continuous positive airway pressure (CPAP), bi-level positive airway pressure (BiPAP), and bag valve mask (BVM) assisted respirations.
- IV antibiotics and hydration generally are not "Comfort-Focused Treatment."
- Treatment of dehydration prolongs life. If a patient desires IV fluids, indicate "Selective Treatment" or "Full Treatment."
- Depending on local EMS protocol, "Additional Orders" written in Section B may not be implemented by EMS personnel.

Reviewing POLST

It is recommended that POLST be reviewed periodically. Review is recommended when:

- The patient is transferred from one care setting or care level to another, or
- There is a substantial change in the patient's health status, or
- The patient's treatment preferences change.

Modifying and Voiding POLST

- A patient with capacity can, at any time, request alternative treatment or revoke a POLST by any means that indicates intent to revoke. It is recommended that revocation be documented by drawing a line through Sections A through D, writing "VOID" in large letters, and signing and dating this line.
- A legally recognized decisionmaker may request to modify the orders, in collaboration with the physician/NP/PA, based on the known desires of the patient or, if unknown, the patient's best interests.

This form is approved by the California Emergency Medical Services Authority in cooperation with the statewide POLST Task Force. For more information or a copy of the form, visit **www.caPOLST.org.**

SEND FORM WITH PATIENT WHENEVER TRANSFERRED OR DISCHARGED

Chapter Fourteen

ADVANCE CARE PLANNING ROAD MAP
END-OF-LIFE PLANNING

"All you need is the plan, the road map, and the courage to press on to your destination."

~ Earl Nightingale

"We call them healthcare decisions, but it is really about values. The emphasis is not on 'what's the matter with you.' The question is, 'what matters to you?'"

~ Kate DeBartolo

The road map on the next pages is a tool to gather information for your advance directive. This road map is not an advance directive. It is not a legal document. Laws vary by state. Your state's advance directive may ask for more information that is not covered in this road map. The following pages will help you get started.

Road Map Tips:

- Some answers may need a lot of thought. Take one section at a time. Take breaks when needed.

- You might have to come back to a question. It is okay to skip questions you do not want to answer.

- Talk to your family, friends, faith community, or care team to help with questions you are not sure about.

- Name a healthcare agent if you do not want to take part in your healthcare decisions. Give this road map to your agent. They may find it helpful.

- Review your road map and your advance directives often. You may need to update them as you get older, if you find out you have a serious illness, or if your health changes for the worse.

Advance Care Road Map

Name:_______________________________________Date:_______________

Part 1: Think About Your Values

Your values, beliefs, fears, and hopes can guide your treatment choices

What gives your life meaning? Check all that apply.

___ My family. List their names:

    Spouse/partner:_________________________________

    Children:_______________________________________

    Grandchildren/great-grandchildren:________________

    Siblings:____

    Parents:____

    Others:____

    My friends. List their names:

    ____

    ____

___My religion/spiritual beliefs. What are your spiritual beliefs?

    ____

    ____

___My passions and hobbies. List them:

____

____

___ My career. What is (or was) your career? What part of your job did you enjoy the most?

____

____

___ Other:

____

____

____

Advance Care Planning Road Map

If you did not list it on the previous page, do you practice a religion?
    ___ yes   ___ no

List your religion, place of worship, and names of trusted spiritual counselors. Or describe your spiritual beliefs if you do not practice a religion.

Do you have religious beliefs that might affect your healthcare choices? Ask a trusted spiritual counselor if you do not know.
    ___ yes   ___ no   ___ I don't know

(Examples: I cannot eat animal products; I cannot receive someone else's blood)

What things or activities do you enjoy?

(Examples: Your favorite music, books, TV shows, movies, sports, flowers, food, hobbies)

What do you fear or dislike? (Examples: Darkness, certain kinds of music, animals, bugs, foods, smells)

What does "quality of life" mean to you? (Examples: Managing pain, spending time with family, doing things I enjoy, living on my own)

Advance Care Planning Road Map

Part 2: Think about your hopes and fears during a serious illness

Your answers will help guide your treatment choices during a serious illness.

Do you have a serious illness now?   ___ yes   ___ no

If "no," it may still help to try to answer some of these questions.

Is there a coming event that you hope to be a part of?

(Examples: Wedding, anniversary, birthday, birth of a grandchild)

Are there things you want to do or projects you want to complete?

(Examples: Visit a special person, finish a quilt, fix the car)

What is on your bucket list? What have you always wanted to try?

(Examples: Travel to a special place, go to a concert, learn how to play an instrument)

Do you have broken relationships you want to mend.

___ yes   ___ no

If "yes," name the person(s). What might you do to reach out?

Advance Care Planning Road Map

What else to you hope for that might make you feel at peace?

Examples: Visit from a spiritual counselor, knowing my family will be okay, finding a home for my pet.

Name friends or loved ones who might be able to help you complete tasks.

Name:____

Phone number:________________________________

Name: ____

Phone number:________________________________

Name: ____

Phone number:________________________________

What do you fear about having a serious illness? Check all that apply.

_____ Being in pain

_____ Not being able to walk or get around by myself

_____ Not being able to breathe on my own

_____ Not being able to go to church or practice my spiritual beliefs.

_____ Not being able to talk

____ Not being able to do things I enjoy

____ Being on life support

____ Being a burden to loved ones

____ Staying in a hospital

____ Living in a nursing home

____ Not knowing who loved ones are

____ Not being able to work

____ Not knowing who I am

____ Being alone

____ Not being able to take care of my
loved ones

____ Not being able to live on my own

____ Not being able to take care of myself (eat, bathe, get
dressed, etc.)

____ Dying

____ Other:

Advance Care Planning Road Map

What are the top 3 most important things for you to get from medical care while you are seriously ill? Number them 1 (most important) to 3:

____ Live as long as possible

____ Increase my quality of life

____ Manage pain and symptoms

____ Emotional, social, and/or spiritual support

____ Emotional, social, and/or spiritual support for my loved ones and caregivers

____ Other:

____ Other:

____ Other:

Doctor(s) you want to be involved in your care, if possible:

Name:____

Phone:________________________

Address:____

Name:____

Phone:________________________

Address:____

Hospital(s) you prefer, if possible:

Hospital:___________________________________

Phone:___________________________

Address:_______________________________________

Hospital:___________________________________

Phone:___________________________

Address:_______________________________________

If you need ongoing care to meet your wishes, how will you pay for it? Check all that apply. Ask your care team what your payment options may cover.

___Private health insurance

___Pay out of pocket

___Medicare

___I don't know

___Medicaid

___Other

Advance Care Planning Road Map

Part 3: Name your healthcare agent

This person will speak for you if you cannot speak for yourself.

This section will help you fill out your durable power of attorney for health care.

Remember to check your state's laws regarding healthcare agents.
___ I do not want to name a healthcare agent. I will let my family, care team, and/or state courts decide what is best for me (skip to the next page).

My FIRST choice for healthcare agent:

Name: ________________________________

Phone: ____________________________

Address:____

This person is my:

___ Parent   ___ Spouse/partner   ___ Child (18/19 years +)

___ Sibling   ___ Friend

Other:

My BACKUP choice for healthcare agent:

Name: ________________________________

Phone: ____________________________

Address:____

This person is my:

___ Parent   ___ Spouse/partner   ___ Child (18/19 years +)

___ Sibling   ___ Friend

Other:

Have you already asked these people to be your agent?

___ yes   ___ no

How much flexibility will your agent have in making healthcare decisions for you?

> Some people feel strongly about their choices and do not allow flexibility. Others allow flexibility, trusting their agent to make the best choice at the time.

___Full: My agent and care team can change my wishes if they think that is best for me.

___Some: My agent can change my wishes EXCEPT these:

____
____
____
____

___None: My agent must follow my wishes EXACTLY if it is reasonably possible.

Advance Care Planning Road Map

Part 4: Learn about your illness

Learning about your illness and treatment options can prepare you for what may be ahead. It may still be helpful to fill out some parts of this section even if you are not sick.

How much do you want to know about your illness and treatment?

> Not everyone wants to know all about their illness. Each person has a different comfort level with how much they want to know.

> ___Nothing: Skip to Part 5.

> ___Some things: I just want basic information.

> ___Everything: I want to know all of the details.

What do you know about your illness and treatment?

> Fill in what you know, based on what you care team has told you. If you do not know something, do you want to know about it? Check what applies to you. Share this with your care team. They can give you more information if needed.

Diagnosis (the name of your illness):

____

> ___ I don't know this, but I'd like to know

> ___ I don't want to know this

Symptoms (including ones you don't have yet):

___ I don't know this, but I'd like to know

___ I don't want to know this

Prognosis (how the illness will likely affect you, now and in the future):

___ I don't know this, but I'd like to know

___ I don't want to know this

Life expectancy how long you might have left to live:

___ I don't know this, but I'd like to know

___ I don't want to know this

Treatments suggested by your care team:

___ I don't know this, but I'd like to know

___ I don't want to know this

Caregiving and support needs (such as transfer to a hospital, therapy, home care, palliative care, assisted living, nursing home, home health care, hospice care):

Support you will need now:

___ I don't know this, but I'd like to know

___ I don't want to know this

Support you will need in the future:

_____ I don't know this, but I'd like to know

_____ I don't want to know this

What other questions do you have about your illness or treatment?

What else do you NOT want to know?

Advance Care Planning Road Map

Part 5: Think about treatments during a serious illness

Talk to your care team about treatments that might apply to you during your illness.

Common treatments are described in this section. If a treatment might apply to you, check "Yes" if you want it or "No" if you do not. Spaces to write-in other treatments your care team suggests are on the next page.

You can add a copy of this section to your advance directive. Ask your care team to add a copy to your medical record or POLST form.

Treatments during a serious illness or near the end may…

…be a good fit if they:	…NOT be a good fit if they:
___Relieve pain and suffering discomfort	___Cause pain or other
___Increase quality of life life	___Decrease quality of life
___Are in line with your values your values	___Are not in line with
___Improve function with no other benefit	___Only keep you alive

Blood transfusions: Donated blood is injected into your body. Replaces lost blood. May treat some diseases. Some religions do not support this. Some side effects: back pain, dizziness, fever, shortness of breath.

___ Yes   ___ No   ___ I don't know

Chemotherapy: Strong drugs are injected into the body to kill cancer cells. May shrink tumors. Some side effects: feeling weak or tired, hair loss, bruising, bleeding, nausea, vomiting, weight loss.

___ Yes   ___ No   ___ I don't know

Dialysis: A machine filters waste from the blood if your kidneys fail. (Treatment without a machine is possible for fewer patients). Minor surgery is needed to prepare for treatment. Treatment takes many hours and must be done on a routine, ongoing schedule. Dialysis is not a cure. Some side effects: low blood pressure, nausea vomiting, a feeling of fullness in the belly.

___Yes   ___No   ___I don't know

Invasive tests: Such as biopsies or blood tests. Collects body tissues to test for disease. Tests may be painful. Many need surgery. Some risks: bleeding, infection.

___ Yes   ___ No   ___ I don't know

Pacemaker or implanted defibrillator: A device is placed in your chest or belly with surgery. It keeps your heartbeat steady or shocks your heart if it stops. Some risks: bleeding, bruising, infection; damage to blood vessels, nerves, lungs; pain/burdens at the end of life.

___ Yes   ___ No   ___ I don't know

Radiation therapy: Beams of intense energy kill cancer cell. May shrink tumors. Some side effects: feeling tired, red/peeling skin, soreness, nausea, vomiting, hair loss.

___ Yes   ___ No   ___ I don't know

Sedation: Drugs calm you or put you into a sleep-like state. Relieves extreme pain or unrest. Some side effects after sedation: feeling tired, headache, nausea.

___ Yes   ___ No   ___ I don't know

Surgery: The body is cut open to repair/remove tissues, organs, or bones. May need anesthesia, intubation, or a ventilator. Some side effects: feeling tired or weak, loss of appetite, bruising, swelling, numbness. Risks: pain, bleeding, infection, added burden near end of life.

___ Yes   ___ No   ___ I don't know

X-rays, PET/CT/CAT scans, MRIs: Images are taken of the inside of the body. Can show how an illness has progressed. Often painless. Will expose you to low beams of radiation or magnetic/radio waves. Some side effects: nausea, headache, dizziness.

___ Yes   ___ No   ___ I don't know

Write other treatments your care team suggests below. Ask about the possible pros and cons of each. Then choose whether or not you want the treatment.

- ✓ Treatment:
  - o Pros
  - o Cons

  ___Yes   ___No   ___I don't know

- ✓ Treatment:
  - o Pros

- o   Cons

___Yes   ___No   ___I don't know

✓ Treatment:

- o   Pros

- o   Cons

___ Yes   ___ No   ___ I don't know

Advance Care Planning Road Map

Part 6: Think about treatments near the end of life

This will help your care team update your medical record or fill out a POLST form if you are seriously ill or near the end of life. This section should be filled out after an in-depth talk with the care team about our values, condition, and goals.

CPR (cardiopulmonary resuscitation): Used if your breathing or heart stops. CPR may combine chest compressions (pushing down hard on the chest), rescue breaths, intubation, electric shocks to the heart, and machine. Risks: being taken to a hospital or ICU; being hooked up to machines; damage to the ribs, lungs, brain, or other organs. Check one:

____ Yes, I want CPR if I am seriously ill or near end of life.

____ No, I do not want CPR if I am seriously ill or near end of life. (As your care team to complete a DNR or a POLST form.

ANH (artificial nutrition and hydration): Feeding tubes give you liquid food if you cannot swallow or feed yourself. Tubes are pushed into the stomach through the nose, mouth, or belly, sometimes with surgery. This can keep you alive, but it will not cure your illness. Risks of feeding tubes: aspiration (getting saliva, vomit, etc., in the lungs), lung infection, other infections, nausea, vomiting, ulcers.

IV's give you fluids and medicine. They are placed with needles. IV fluids near the end of life may cause added pain or discomfort. Check one:

____ Yes, I want ANH if I am seriously ill or near the end of life.

____ No, I do not want ANH if I am seriously ill or near the end of life.

____ I want a time-limited trial of ANH, if approved by my care team.

Your care team might approve a time-limited trial of treatment like ANH. You can try the treatment for a set amount of time. You can keep doing it if it helps. Treatment is stopped if it does not help or causes harm. It might be harder to stop a treatment than to not start it at all.

Medical Interventions: The kind of treatment you want if you cannot communicate and are seriously ill or near the end of life, are breathing, and have a pulse. Check one:

____ **Full Treatment**. Prolong life with all suggested treatments. May include:

- ✓ Intubation – A tube is inserted into your airway or stomach through the nose, mouth, throat, or belly. Some must be placed with surgery.

- ✓ Ventilator – A breathing machine keeps you alive if you cannot breathe on your own. Air is pushed into the lungs through a tube. You will not be able to talk.

- ✓ Transfer to the hospital

- ✓ Transfer to ICU – Intensive care unit. You will often be hooked up to many tubes and machines. Staff watches you closely. Visitors are limited.

- ✓ Treatments listed below, as needed

____ **Limited Treatment**. Basic medical care. Avoids intubation, ventilators, ICU, and added burdens. May include:

- ✓ Antibiotics – Medicine to treat infections. Some side effects: upset stomach, diarrhea.

- ✓ IVs – Gives you fluids and medicine. A small tube is inserted into a vein with a needle.

✓ Heart monitors – Keeps track of heart rate and breathing. A non-painful device is used.

✓ Transfer to the hospital only if needed

✓ Referral to palliative care – A team-approach to care. Treats pain and symptoms. Gives emotional and spiritual support to the patient and family.

✓ Treatments listed below, as needed.

____ **Comfort Measures Only**. Symptom management. Focus on comfort and easing suffering. Avoids transfers to the hospital or ICU. Avoids life-sustaining treatments (CPR, intubation, ventilators). May include:

✓ Medication for pain management – May include opioids such as morphine. Given by mouth, suppository, IV, or injection. Common side effects (which are treated): constipation, itching.

✓ Antibiotics and other medicines to help ease symptoms

✓ Wound care

✓ Oxygen for comfort

✓ Suction – Mucus, saliva, blood, vomit is vacuumed out of the airway. Helps you breathe. May prevent choking.

✓ Transfer to the hospital only if symptoms cannot be managed where you are

✓ Referral to palliative care or hospice care – Hospice care is multi-level care for dying patients with 6 months or less to live.

Advance Care Planning Road Map

Part 7: Think about care you want at the end of life

This section will help you fill out your living will.

Do you want your life prolonged for as long as it is reasonably possible if you are dying or permanently unconscious (in a coma or persistent vegetative state)?

___ Yes   ___ No   ___ I don't know

Do not prolong my life if: Check all that apply:

___ I'm dying (have a terminal illness)   ___   I   have   severe dementia

___ I am permanently unconscious   ___ I have severe brain damage

___ I've been on life support for_____ (days/weeks/months) with no improvement

___ Other:

Do you want a feeding tube/IV fluids if you cannot eat or drink on your own at the end of life?

___ Yes   ___ No   ___ I don't know

Do you want a feeding tube/IV fluids if you are permanently unconscious?

___ Yes   ___ No   ___ I don't know

Where do you hope to spend your last days? Check all that apply.

___ Home   ___Hospital   ___ Nursing home   ___   Assisted living

___ It doesn't matter to me   ___ Other

Where do you NOT want to spend your last days, if possible? Check all that apply.

___Home   ___Hospital   ___ Nursing home   ___   Assisted living

___ It doesn't matter to me   ___ Other

Do you want hospice care if you have a terminal illness? Hospice care treats a dying patient's unique physical, emotional, social, and spiritual needs. Support is given to family and caregivers.

___ Yes   ___ No   ___ I don't know

If your state has a right to die law, is this an option you might want?

___ Yes   ___ No   ___ I don't know

Note: Also known as "medical aid in dying" or "physician-assisted death with dignity." Laws allow some dying patients to get medicine to end their lives. Most states do not have a right to die law. If your state has a right to die law and you check "yes," talk to your doctor. A doctor has the right to refuse this request.

Advance Care Planning Road Map

Other instructions for my health care near the end of life:

Advance Care Planning Road Map

Part 8: Choose donation and other options after death

This part lists options for your body after death. Your state may not offer all these options.

Do you wish to donate organs, tissues, or body parts after you die?

___ Yes   ___ No

If you chose "yes":

___ All organs, tissues, or parts that are needed and can be used

___ Only these organs or parts:

Do you wish to donate your whole body for research after you die?

___ Yes   ___ No

Do you want an autopsy (surgery after death to find out the cause of death)?

___ Yes   ___ No   ___ Only if it is needed by law

After death, I want my body to be:

___ Buried   ___ Cremated   ___ Other

This person should oversee my funeral plans:

___ My agent   ___ Other

Name:_________________________________Phone:_____________________

Funeral home I prefer:

Other instructions to follow my death:

Conclusion

I started writing this book during the coronavirus pandemic. As of this writing there have been 7,000,000 reported cases in the United States with over 200,000 deaths. I am sure these numbers will be much higher before we no longer need to be concerned with COVID-19. I mention these numbers because each one represents a human life. Most of us do not wake up and believe it is our last day on this planet. Even when a person is close to death, it is hard for them to think about the actual moment they will draw their last breath. My point is this, we do not know the time or the hour of our death. Therefore, we should live each day as if is our last. Moreover, you need to be having the appropriate conversations. Remember what I said in Chapter Six.

Hopefully, I have given you food for thought. We all have blindsides. Areas of our character that are less than stellar and hidden from us. We just do not see them. Others probably see them clearly, but they allude us. For that reason, we should welcome personal introspection. We need to examine our conscious thoughts and feelings. From a psychological perspective, this means my personal observation of my mental state. From a spiritual perspective, it means my personal examination of my soul. I encourage you to conduct self-assessment examinations. Think about the footprints you are leaving as you walk through life. It is not a matter of making your path straight without curves, bumps, and potholes. Curves, bumps, and potholes bring insight and purpose. A chance to become stronger. The key is to make sure your feet are well planted as you walk along. When your feet are well planted with each step you are less likely to stumble. And if you do stumble, you will be better equipped to get up and continue your journey. Obviously, this metaphor is describing how to live with less blindsides.

I want you to live well and to die well. I want your death to be the final act of love you give to your family and friends. You accomplish this by leaving nothing to chance regarding your death. Talk about what you want and do not want. Ask for and receive forgiveness where necessary. Do the hard work of reconciliation if needed. And be thankful. Focus on the positive and not the negative of your life. There is no perfect life. We all have regrets. You have read about some of mine. This is why God's grace is so important. Receiving His grace helps you forgive yourself. To leave this life with a sense of peace and readiness, you must be grateful for your life. God's grace gives you freedom to be grateful, regrets and all.

About the Author

Terry W. Barnett, MDiv., J.D., DMin., has worked with the dying for over twenty years. Over the last eleven years, Dr. Barnett has worked as Chaplain for the Rosewood Senior Living Community in Bakersfield, California. Dr. Barnett specializes in end-of-life care and is a sought-after speaker on how to die well. Dr. Barnett holds an undergraduate degree from Oregon State University in Sociology, a Master of Divinity degree from Fuller Theological Seminary, a degree in Juris Prudence from Monterey College of Law, and a doctorate from New York Theological Seminary in end-of-life care. Dr. Barnett lives in Bakersfield, California and enjoys sailing, surfing, and long walks on the beach. He can be reached at dyingwell101@gmail.com.

For more information on Dr. Barnett and Dying Well 101 go to **www.dyingwell101.com.**

Resources

Dying Well 101: www.dyingwell101.com
This site provides important and practical insights on how to achieve a good death. It focuses on forgiveness, reconciliation, and having a sense of gratitude. These three concepts play an important role in feeling ready to pass from this life.

The Conversation Project: www.theconversationproject.org.
Resources focused on helping people talk about their wishes and values for end-of-life care.

Aspire: www.aspirehealthcare.com.
Information about specialized physician practices that provide comprehensive medical care in the home. Particularly for patients facing serious illness.

Elisabeth Kubler-Ross Foundation: www.ekrfoundation.org.
This foundation carries on the great work of Dr. Kubler-Ross, an end-of-life pioneer.

End of Life University: www.eoluniversity.com.
This site consists of in-depth educational interviews with experts covering all areas of end of life.

Meet Grace: www.meetgrace.com.
An online hospice and assisted living directory.

The Order of the Good Death: www.orderofthegooddeath.com.
A group of funeral industry professionals, academics, and artists exploring ways to prepare a death-phobic culture for their inevitable mortality.

Recompose: www.recompose.life.
Recompose is developing a process that converts human remains into soil so that we can nourish new life after we die. Recompositing is an alternative to cremation and conventional burial.

Future File: www.futurefile.com
A comprehensive and easy-to-use system for legacy planning.

Everplans: www.everplans.com.
A secure, digital archive of wills, trusts, and insurance policies; important accounts and passwords; advance directives and DNRs; final wishes and funeral preferences.

Death Over Dinner: www.deathoverdinner.org.
A website that includes everything you need to begin and host a conversation over dinner about end-of-life issues.

GYST: www.gyst.com
An online service that helps you get your end-of-life documents in order. Includes will, living will/advance directive, and life insurance.

Additional Literary Resources

Michael Appleton and Todd Henschell, *At Home with Terminal Illness: A Family Guide to Hospice in the Home.* Englewood Cliffs, N.J.: Prentice-Hall, 1995.

Sandra L. Bertman, *Facing Death:Images, Insights, and Intervention.* Bristol, Penn: Taylor & Francis, 1991.

Charles Corr, Clyde Nabe, and Donna Corr, *Death and Dying, Life and Living.* Pacific Grove, Calif.: Brooks/Cole Publishing, 1994.

David Feinstein and Peg Elliott Mayo, *Rituals for Living and Dying.* New York: Harper-Collins, 1990.

Andrea Sankar, *Dying at Home.* Baltimore: Johns Hopkins University Press, 1991.

Sidney Wanzer and Joseph Glenmullen, *To Die Well.* Philadelphia, PA: Da Capo Press, 2007.

Steve Gordon and Irene Kacandes, *Let's Talk About Death.* New York: Prometheus Books, 2015.

Ira Byock, *Dying Well: Peace and Possibilities at the End of Life.* New York: Riverhead Books, 1997.

Atul Gawande, *Being Mortal.* New York: Picador, 2014.

Henri Nouwen, *Our Greatest Gift: A Meditation on Dying and Caring.* New York: HarperCollins Publishers, 1994.

Henri Nouwen, *Spiritual Direction.* New York: HarperCollins Publishers, 2006.

John Dunlop, *Finishing Well to the Glory of God.* Wheaton, Illinois: Crossway, 2011.

Maggie Callanan, *Final Journeys: A practical guide for bringing care and comfort at the end of life.* New York: Bantam Dell, 2008.

Notes

Chapter Five

[1] Nancy J. Duff, *Making Faithful Decisions at the End of Life* (Louisville, Kentucky: Westminster John Knox Press, 2018), 2.

[2] Elisabeth Kubler-Ross, *On Death and Dying* (New York: Simon & Schuster, 2014), 6.

[3] Kubler-Ross, *On Death and Dying*, 7.

[4] Miltiades, Helen. "*Advancing Palliative Care in California.*" Lecture, Using Palliative Care, Bakersfield, January 31, 2018.

[5] Henri J.M. Nouwen, *Life of the Beloved* (New York: Crossroads Publishing Company, 1992), 118.

[6] Megory Anderson, *Sacred Dying* (New York: Marlowe & Company, 2003), 121.

[7] Henri J.M. Nouwen, *Befriending Death* (New York: Orbis Books, 2009), 85.

[8] David Kessler, *The Needs of the Dying* (New York: HarperCollins, 1997), 112.

[9] Henri J.M. Nouwen, *Befriending Death* (New York: Orbis Books, 2009), 87.

[10] These studies include: S.M. Holmes, M.W. Rabow, S.L. Dibble, "Screening the Soul: Communication Regarding Spiritual Concerns among Primary Care Physicians and Seriously Ill Patients Approaching the End of Life," *American Journal of Hospice and Palliative Medicine* 23, no. 1 (January – February 2006): 25-31; D.B. Hinshaw, "Spiritual Issues in Surgical Palliative Care," *Surgical Clinics of North America* 85, no. 2 (1999): 257-72; K.E. Steinhauser et al., "In Search of a Good Death: Observations of Patients, Families and Providers," *Annals of Internal Medicine* 132, no. 10 (May 16, 2000): 825-32.

[11] Kubler-Ross, *On Death and Dying, 37-109.*

[12] Kubler-Ross, *On Death and Dying, 13.*

[13] Gallup Institute, *Spiritual Concerns of American*, 34-35.

[14] I call this the murky darkness of death. Movies and books often portray death as a place of darkness. I am sure this is because of the finality aspect of death. Notwithstanding the theological aspect of death, death is not the absence of light. It is the absence of presence. At death you are no longer in the physical reality you have known throughout your life. You are in a new reality. During those final weeks or days there is a new reality that begins. It is a reality that is murky and shadowy and uncertain. This reality brings with it high anxiety and fear. Even though the body is still alive, emotions and psychological functions of the human brain are without understanding.

[15] The Conversation Project National Survey, (2013).

[16] Ira Byock, M.D., *The Four Things that Matter Most*: Quotes Sogyal Rinpoche, *The Tibetan Book of Living and Dying* (New York, NY: Simon & Schuser, 2014), 37.

[17] Karen Swartz, M.D., *Forgiveness: Your health depends on it*, Johns Hopkins Medicine (https://www.hopkinsmedicine.org/.../forgiveness-your-health-depends-on-it).

[18] E. Erikson, *Identity and the life cycle* (New York: International Universities Press, 1959).

[19] R.N. Bulter, MI Lewis, *Aging and Mental Health* (St Louis, LA: C.V. Mosby, 1982).

Chapter Six

[20] Ram Dass, *Still Here: Embracing Aging, Changing, and Dying* (New York, NY, 2000), 149.

[21] Kubler-Ross, *On Death and Dying*, 7.

[22] Henri J.M. Nouwen, *Befriending Death* (New York: Orbis Books, 2009), 87.

[23] Angelo E. Volandes, *The Conversation* (New York: Bloombury Publishing, 2016), 29

Chapter Seven

[24] Ivan Urli, *Victimhood, Vengefulness, and the Culture of Forgiveness* (Nova Science Publishers, Inc.,2013), 160.

[25] Lewis B. Smedes, *The Art of Forgiving: When you need to forgive and don't know how* (Nashville: Moorings/Random House, 1996), 177-178.

[26] K.A. Koch, H.D. Rodeffer, R.L. Wears, *Changing patterns of terminal care management in an intensive care unit.* Critical Care Med., 1994; 22:233-43.

[27] Daniel Callahan, *The Troubled Dream of Life: In Search of a Peaceful Death* (Washington, DC, Georgetown University Press, 1993), 149-151.

[28] Lewis B. Smedes, *The Art of Forgiving: When you need to forgive and don't know how* (Nashville: Moorings/Random House, 1996), 177-178.

[29] Gospel of John, Chapter 1, verse 12. New Living Transition.

[30] Gospel of Matthew, Chapter 6, verse 44, New Living Transition.

[31] John Dunlop, *Finishing Well to the Glory of God* (Wheaton, Illinois: Crossway,2011), 119.

[32] P. Singer, D. Martin, and M. Kelner, "Quality End-of-Life Care: Patient's Perspective," *Journal of the American Medical Association* 281 (April 28, 1999):163-68.

Chapter Eight

[33] Romans, Chapter 12, verse 18, New Living Translation

Chapter Nine

[34] Ira Byock, M.D., *The Four Things That Matter Most* (New York: Simon & Schuster, 2014), 26.

[35] Romans, Chapter 8, verse 28, New King James Version

Chapter Ten

[36] Geraldine Piorkowski, *Too Close for Comfort: Exploring the Risks of Intimacy.* (Perseus Publishers, Massachusetts, 2007), 89.

[37] Brene Brown, (2011, January) *The Power of Vulnerability*. Retrieved from http://TED.com (Youtube).

Chapter Eleven

[38] Apostle Paul, 2 Corinthians, Chapter 5, verse 19. New Living Translation.

[39] William D. Mounce, *Complete Expository Dictionary of Old and New Testament Words* (Zondervan, MI, 2006), 565.

[40] Gospel of Matthew, Chapter 5, verses 23-24. New King James Version.

[41] Apostle Paul, Colossians, Chapter 3, verses 15-17. New Living Translation.

[42] Apostle Paul, Colossians, Chapter 4, verse 2, New Living Translation.

[43] William D. Mounce, *Complete Expository Dictionary of the Old and New Testament Words* (Zondervan, Michigan, 2006), 721.

[44] Mounce, *Complete Expository Dictionary of the Old and New Testament Words* (Zondervan, Michigan, 2006), 722.

[45] Apostle Paul, 1 Thessalonians, Chapter 5, verses 16-18, New Living Translation.

[46] Psalm of David, Psalm 100, New Living Translation.

[47] Ernest Becker, *The Denial of Death* (New York: Free Press (Simon & Schuster, 1973), 36.

Chapter Twelve

[48] www.healthline.com

[49] J.M. Teno, B.R. Clarridge, et al., "Family Perspectives on End-of-Life Care at the Last Place of Care," *Journal of the American Medical Association* 291 (2004): 88-93. Study from: Center for Gerontology and Health Care Research, Brown Medical School and Department of Community Health, Brown University, Providence, RI; and the Center for Survey Research, University of Massachusetts at Boston.

[50] Daniel Callahan. Death, Mourning and Medical Progress (Washington, DC: Georgetown University Press, 1998), 107.

[51] Margaret Mohrmann, *Medicine as Ministry* (Cleveland: Pilgrim Press, 1995), 13.

[52] Ibid., 16.

[53] Union Pacific Railway Co v. Botsford, 141 US 250, 251 (1891).

[54] Phillip M. Kleespies, *Life and Death Decisions: Psychological and Ethical Considerations in End-of-Life Care* (Washington, D.C.: American Psychological Association, 2004), 34.

[55] *Schloendorff v. Society of New York Hospital*, 211 NY 125, 105 NE 92 (1914).

[56] J. Luce and A. Alpers, End-of-Life Care: What Do the American Courts Say?" *Critical Care Medicine* 29, no. 2 Suppl (2001): N41.

www.ingramcontent.com/pod-product-compliance
Lightning Source LLC
Chambersburg PA
CBHW071559030726
47593CB00001BA/238